To Dr. Jacob R. Marcus

דרישת שלום חם בב

and much esteem

Gerald Cohen

Oct/72

SHIELDING THE FLAME

Other Books by Beryl D. Cohon

Introduction to Judaism
A Book for Jewish Youth

The Prophets: Their Personalities and Teachings

Feasts of the Lord
A sacred pageant

Judaism — In Theory and Practice

From Generation to Generation

Jacob's Well: Some Jewish Sources and Parallels to the Sermon On the Mount

Out of the Heart: Intimate Talks from a Jewish Pulpit on the Personal Issues of Life

God's Angry Men
A Student's Introduction to the Hebrew Prophets

My King and My God: Intimate Talks On the Devotions of Life

Vision and Faith: Confirmation Services for Jewish Congregations

Men at the Crossroads
*Between Jerusalem and Rome,
Synagogue and Church
Lives, Time and Doctrines of the Founders of Rabbinic Judaism and New Testament Christianity*

SHIELDING THE FLAME

A personal and spiritual inventory
of a Liberal Rabbi

by Beryl D. Cohon

BLOCH PUBLISHING COMPANY
NEW YORK

Copyright © 1972

by

Beryl D. Cohon

Library of Congress Catalog Card Number: 72-4801
I.S.B.N.: 0-8197-0293-5

Printed in United States of America

To the Men, Women and Children
of the Congregation of
TEMPLE SINAI
Brookline, Massachusetts

a community of friends —
in appreciation of many years of
happy association, striving to
fulfill the rabbinic precept "to
learn and to teach," this book is
dedicated as an offering of
thanksgiving.

The capital secret of [the preacher's] profession is to convert life into truth. . . . The true preacher can be known by this, that he deals out to the people his life — life passed through the fire of thought.

Ralph Waldo Emerson
Divinity School Address

✡ *Preface*

THE sermons and addresses comprising the present volume were given from the pulpit of Temple Sinai, Brookline, Massachusetts. The sermons were spoken on the High Holy Days since 1964, and are motivated by the emphasis on personal spiritual inventory; the addresses were delivered on special occasions in the history of the congregation since 1939 and seek to define the controlling purposes of a liberal Jewish congregation within the framework of American democracy. It is hoped, by this publication, to recall the vision that beckoned to the Rabbi and the dynamics of the covenant that bound him to his people.

At a time when our altars are desecrated and strange fires are raging; when the Eternal Light in our synagogues flickers and preachers of God's word speak in frustration and fury; when men in the pulpits and the pews are bewildered and sorely tried; when, further, the relationships between Rabbis and congregations are in turmoil, the author dares to hope that some bit of encouragement may issue from these pages for a number of colleagues and congregations on the American scene.

The author is deeply indebted to the congregation of Temple Sinai for the constant encouragement it gave him over the years. The present compilation is the thank offering to all his friends, in the congregation and in the larger community.

He is especially grateful, further, to a good number of friends who have urged him to publish these pulpit offerings in book form and have made it possible for him to do so. Abraham S. Burack and Mrs. Bernard Madfis of The Writer, Inc., were most generous with their skills and time in the production of this book. My profoundest thanks.

Shalom uvracha — peace and blessing!

Beryl D. Cohon

Contents

	Preface	vii

PERSONAL SERMONS

I	After Fifty Years — A Rabbi's Pulpit Confessions	3
II	Where Are You?	13
III	How Tall Are You?	21
IV	Are You Listening?	30
V	When the Foundations Are Destroyed, What Can the Righteous Do?	39
VI	Let Not Arrogance Come Out of Your Mouth	50
VII	A Lamp Unto Our Feet	60
VIII	The Mistress and the Maid	63
IX	A Prayer for Our Country	71
X	Pollution — of Heart and Mind	82

INSTITUTIONAL

XI	Dedicating a Synagogue	95
XII	A Heap of Witness	100
XIII	Thy Vows Are Upon Me, O God	110
XIV	Dedicating a School House: Plant Your Sappling	113
	Epilogue: I am the Synagogue	117

PERSONAL SERMONS

1

After Fifty Years: A Rabbi's Pulpit Confessions
[5733-1972]

THIS Rosh Hashanah morning, by the grace of God — and the sufferance of congregations — I am privileged to give my fiftieth consecutive New Year sermon. Back in 1922 Hebrew Union College sent me to Trinidad, Colorado, to conduct High Holy Day services for a small congregation, Temple Aaron. I had been admitted to the College and was scheduled to begin my rabbinic studies that fall, but had not yet attended a single class session. Dr. Julian Morgenstern, the President of the College, and a friend of the family, must have been hard put to press into service a naive, inexperienced youngster. Since then, year after year, for half a century — in Trinidad, Colorado; Pensacola, Florida; Cumberland, Maryland; Boston, and, of course, with you here in Brookline — have I had the deep experience of leading congregations in High Holy Day worship and trying to bring "a message." Looking back over the fifty years, in the solemnity of our Rosh Hashanah worship, I find it a humbling and awesome experience. Earnestly I ask you to unite your hearts with mine in our traditional benediction:

boruch atto adonoi elohenu melech ho'olom shehecheyonu v'kiy'monu v'higionu lazman hazzeh Praised be Thou, Lord our God, Master of the universe, who has kept us alive and sustained us and brought us to this season.

Some cherished friends and colleagues in the building of our congregation I miss badly this morning. I recall them for blessing. *zichronom livrocho.*

What shall I talk about this morning, this morning of my golden jubilee?

Celebrating my fiftieth consecutive Rosh Hashanah sermon, I want to talk to you about the sermon as the Rabbi's unique instrument. Just what is a sermon? What has it meant in the life of the Synagogue over the centuries? What has it meant in the lives of generations upon generations of Rabbis, who poured their lives into it as their special means of perpetuating, strengthening, fortifying Judaism in their times? What has the sermon meant — what must it mean — in the lives of men, women and children under a Rabbi's guidance?

I want to take you into my confidence this morning and talk to you on what the sermon has meant in my life as Rabbi, what I have understood the sermon to mean, what I have tried to do with it. The neglect of the sermon on the part of congregations and — alas! — too many Rabbis, I am profoundly convinced, is one of the tragedies of Jewish life today.

I know it is not a popular subject, but earnestly I ask you: please hear me out. You who have been so patient with me over the years will be patient once again.

I must speak categorically, in competition as I am with that clock on the wall.

FIRST, I must convey to you a historic fact in Judaism. It is primary to an understanding and primary to any sort of intelligent appreciation of the sermon.

The rabbinic masters who shaped our Judaism insist

that God gave Moses on Mount Sinai *two* torahs: the *Written*, the Five Books of Moses and, later, the rest of the Bible; and an *Oral* torah — the interpretations and expansions of the Written, thus stretching the Written to meet every contingency in life, making it vibrant with and equal to the challenges of life and the times. This Oral torah consists of a vast literature: Bible exposition, laws, legends, comprising the entire "vast sea of the Talmud" and much more. Without this Oral tradition Judaism shrinks into a brittle parchment, a dead, ossified, legalistic creed. Our masters have a technical term for it: *torah sheb'al peh*.

To reach the humble masses, the men and women who would not or could not busy themselves in the life of the academies, or were not equal to their stringent intellectual disciplines, they developed the *drush*, the sermon — popular, often highly fanciful, expositions of Bible text. They aimed at the humble, everyday people at their humble everyday work. They sought to invest their lives with Torah, with sanctity, with sacred learning, with vision, capturing their imaginations and captivating their emotions. The sermon has been, age after age, the unique instrument in the hands of the popular teachers of Judaism. It has had an enormous influence. The Church borrowed this instrument from the so-called Pharisees and gave it a new emphasis. Jesus and Paul used it magnificently. They were supreme preachers. The humble sermon was their special instrument, borrowed from the earliest rabbinic masters, and it made Christianity a living, compelling, world-conquering faith.

Torah is more than an ancient scroll, more than a learned disquisition, more than a theology, more than history, more than an ancient literature; Torah is a vibrant, challenging, exalted and exalting faith. It is the living word of the living God, and the sermon has been the pitcher at the well of living waters.

A distinguished historian, the newly-elected President of the Jewish Theological Seminary, Dr. Gerson D. Cohen, wrote some years ago: "Only the sermon . . . has made of the Bible a living book rather than a literary classic merely for pleasure and edification."

"Let not the humble sermon be a trivial matter in your estimation," the rabbinic masters plead with us, "for by means of the humble sermon man finds his God." In their unique and charming manner, the synagogue preachers say, When a King drops a precious pearl, how does he go about searching for it in the dark if not with the help of a penny candle?

My friends, I have striven to keep the penny candle burning in some dark hours. Have not all of us lived through black nights — world wars, Hitler, murder, dispersion, concentration camps, crematoria, horror upon horror? And have not all of us lived through personal sorrows, and the pain of the years? We have drained the bitter cup of life and have staggered and reeled at times, even more violently than the ancient apocalyptists imagined in their delirium. Many of you came to the Temple on the Sabbaths and holy days seeking a bit of cheer and vision. I felt I owed you a drink of cold water from the living well of our ancient faith.

SECOND. The sermon issues from the life of the preacher, shaped and tempered by his personality, and is aimed at the heart and mind of the worshiper. It does not come out of an ancient text or the latest novel or the latest column in the morning newspaper; it is not a learned discourse and not a smart analysis. The Bible with its tremendous cargo of great texts, the popular writings of our time — novel or essay or drama or biography — are vital for the preacher to feed his own mind and soul. Rabbis who are not immersed in great literature, in one form or another, dry up and shrivel on the inside. They are empty men making a noisy fuss.

The primary source of a Rabbi's sermon — if he has any vital vision and a bit of wisdom in his life — is his own inner life, his own living and striving, sorrowing and rejoicing. The abundance of his heart and mind is the source of his sermons.

On a cold, snowy winter afternoon, on a Sabbath, in 1838, Ralph Waldo Emerson was in his pew, worshiping with his congregation in Concord. He watched the snow falling, heard the minister drone his sermon, and it came over him that the snow was real and beautiful but the preacher and his sermon were only spectral. There was nothing real about the man, nothing human in what he was saying. He was tempted to go to church no more, he recalls. He affirms, in dead earnestness:

> The capital secret of [the preacher's] profession, namely, to convert life into truth, he had not learned . . . The true preacher can be known by this, that he deals out to the people his life — life passed through the fire of thought.

This conception of the sermon gripped me and has held me captive over the years.

A sermon is not an exposition of a Bible text as such, not a prophecy of things to come, not an analysis of religion in the abstract, not a rehearsal of philosophy or literature as such. These have their honored places in the intellectual life of the modern synagogue. A synagogue deprived of these areas of culture and learning is intellectually bankrupt, alienating the mentally alert. A sermon is a preacher sharing with his friends, the congregation, some wisdom for living he has wrung from the years.

I recall an experience when I was serving a congregation in Cumberland, Maryland, in the early years of my rabbinate, before I came under the spell of Emerson's teaching. I had given a talk from the pulpit on a Sabbath eve on Solomon ibn Gabirol, the great synagogue poet of eleventh century Spain. Surely Gabirol was a legitimate subject. We still sing his hymns. He was probably the greatest synagogue poet of all time. After the service, a member of the congregation said to me that what I had said was "far, far away." It didn't mean anything to him; it had not touched his life. He had his problems, as do all men — problems with his family, with his business; he was growing older and anxieties come to all of us with the advancing years. He came to his temple to workship on the Sabbath eve and enjoy the fellowship of his friends. And what did I give him? A discourse on a dead poet, of whom he had never heard and would in all probability never hear again. He couldn't care less. "It was so far, far away."

It stuck in my mind, and I have felt its prick again and again. A sermon comes from the heart of the preacher and is a sharing of whatever little wisdom he may have acquired from his living and thinking and aspiring, rejoicing and sorrowing. I have felt over the years that if I could not do that I had no business in the pulpit.

The great issues of our time — war? racism? human exploitation? poverty? housing? busing?. Should not the Rabbi preach on these? Of course! Of course! "Cry aloud, spare not, lift up your voice like a trumpet, and declare to my people their sins. . . ." We rehearse this prophetic teaching on Yom Kippur. Judaism without a concern with these burning issues of our time is fraudulent. But, for the Rabbi in his pulpit, these social issues must be unfinished personal business; he must declare himself on these, but not in the manner of the statistician, nor the politician, nor the journalist, nor in the manner of the agitator. They must come as compelling personal convictions aimed at the intelligent and sincere men and women in the pews.

THIRD. What is the primary purpose of a sermon? Why do we preach from pulpits, and knock ourselves out (and knock out congregations)? The answer is implied in what I have said; I am making a special point of it for the sake of emphasis and clarity.

There are different types of sermons, and the preacher — if he knows his business — will use all of them. The harp of faith has many strings, and the preacher who keeps plucking on one string all the time is bound to be boring and futile. The primary aim of preaching, over the years of a Rabbi's life with his congregation, is to nurture the thirsty soul — to refresh, to strengthen, to fortify, to keep alive soul and conscience.

Nikos Kazantzakis, in his brilliant book, "Report to Greco," recalls the story of a Mohammedan mystic trapped in a desert. The sun and sand and wind were merciless; he was perishing. He was delirious in his need for water. He finally drags himself to a well; lowers his little bucket, and pulls it up. It is filled with gold! He empties the gold into the burning sand and lowers his bucket again. He pulls it up. It is filled with silver. He dumps the silver into the thirsty sand and tries once more. He speaks a prayer. "I know you are full of treasures, Lord, but just give me some water to drink. I am thirsty; I am perishing for want of water!"

This is the business of the religious pulpit, badly neglected in our time. Sermons on behalf of justice, peace, attacking the vicious, exposing the corrupt — of course! But who will nurture the tender plant of faith in the weary heart? Who will speak a healing word to the pained and crushed, the bewildered, the bereaved, if not the man of

God in his pulpit? Where may a man's conscience be roused and his vision cleared if not in his sanctuary?

Yes, water, clear water for the thirsty soul! Or, to change the metaphor, good preaching is placing a flashlight in the hands of a man lost on a dark night when the lights are out for him — a little flashlight helping him find his way home to his loved ones, and to find himself.

FINALLY, I read a poem by way of conclusion. It is not much as poetry, perhaps not poetry at all; but it does have a great deal of common sense, and helps me summarize what I have been trying to say to you. (I regret I can not give you the author's name; I have not been able to find it.)

> When I was young and fancy free,
> My folks had no fine clothes for me.
> All I got was words:
>
> > Gott zu danken — Thank God;
> > Gott wet geben — God will provide;
> > Zoll men nor leben un sein Gezunt —
> > We should only live and be healthy.
>
> When I was wont to travel far,
> They didn't provide me with a car.
> All I got was words:
>
> > Geh gezunt — Go in health;
> > Geh pamelach — Go carefully;
> > Hab a glikliche reize — Have a safe trip.
>
> I wanted to increase my knowledge,
> But they couldn't send me to college.
> All I got was words:
>
> > Hab seichel — Have common sense,
> > Zei nicht ken nahr — Don't be a fool.
> > Toire is die beste schoire,
> > Learning is its own best reward.

The years have flown, the world has turned,
Things I've forgotten, things I've learned,
Yet I remember:

> Zag dem emes — Tell the truth;
> Gib tzedakah — Be charitable;
> Hab rachmonus — Have compassion;
> Zei a mentch — Be a "mentch."

All I got was words.

Nothing but words?

Last year I read and discarded heaps of my sermons collected over the years. I have been in the habit of writing out my pulpit talks. And I have been brooding: What have I given my friends in the pews? Nothing but words?

Perhaps, in the dry spells in the life of a Rabbi and in the life of a congregant, sermons may — and too often do — add up to nothing but words. But there were key words in all these sermons, brave, exalted and exalting words:

GOD, the Holy One of Israel, blessed be His Name. LOVE, love of God and love of man. FAITH, yes even in our time — Hitler, Auschwitz, millions of men and women crushed, going up the crematoria chimneys. Nevertheless, faith! "Though He slay me, yet will I trust in Him!" "The righteous liveth by his faith." If we could "prove" the existence of God, square His being with our petty logic, He would not be God. Faith is a heroic, triumphant attitude to life and all its blinding blows. "Yea, though I walk through the valley of the shadow of death I shall fear no evil, for Thou art with me!" YISGADAL V'ISKADASH SHME RABBAH. "Exalted and magnified be His Great Name." I have stood by the open graves of loved ones with many of you, and together we recited these words. Only words? I have led many of you, and children and grandchildren of many of you, in the marriage vows: "Be you

CONSECRATED unto me...." Nothing but words? How shallow and how cynical can we be?

I close with two more words: SHALOM UVRACHA, and on this Rosh Hashanah morning I add two more words: SHANAH TOVA! A good year and long life to all of you.

2

Where Are You?
[5726-1965]

THE master word in the observance of the High Holy Days — in practical, everyday English — is *inventory,* spiritual inventory; in the more elevated language of our tradition, *heshban hanefesh,* stocktaking of the soul. I hope this term is familiar to you. This morning is the twenty-seventh Rosh Hashanah morning that I have been privileged to talk from this pulpit, and year after year after year have I striven to make real the meaning of the Holy Days in terms of personal stocktaking, *heshban hanefesh.*

Businessmen know how imperative stocktaking is in their business. They would not stay in business very long if they did not take accurate inventory at least once a year.

Annually come the Days of Awe and summon us to check the debits and credits in our personal lives, in our family relations, in our communal integration. Nobody can do that for us. We cannot hire an accountant to check our personal worth as men and women, as husbands and wives, as fathers and mothers, as sons and daughters, as responsible Jews in the household of Israel, as constructive citizens in a world caught in the eye of the hurricane. Every responsible soul must look within and check the score in full realization of the shadow on the dial. We Jews make no confession to an intermediary; we confess to God alone in the secret places of our own hearts. That is one of the strengths — and one of the weaknesses — of our faith. Thoughtful, sensitive people can and do have a profound experience in the Jewish version of confession; shallow, thoughtless people find little or no reality in it.

This morning, then, in the quiet of our worship, with the words of the Torah, the penitential chants — rendered so meaningfully by our choir — with the sounds of the *shofar* fresh in our consciousness, I invite you to look inward, reflect, and pronounce judgments on yourselves. It is a sacred confidence between every soul and God. All the Rabbi can do — and all he has the right to do — and that is his duty to do — is to encourage the men and women before him to think through the fabric of their lives and make high resolves.

It would help coordinate our thinking if we held ourselves within the framework of a text. That is the purpose of a text, as every competent preacher knows: a spur and a guide, saving him from rambling and confusion.

I lift a text from the story of Adam and Eve and the Garden of Eden.

I would not blame you if you smiled, a bit amused: How simpleminded can a Rabbi be? In our day, when the earth is rocking under our feet with atomic violence, when nations are in turmoil, and our country is involved in a war in the jungles of Asia, when our sons are once again called to the colors, when every city and town in the land is in the throes of racial violence or juvenile lawlessness, a Rabbi stands up in his pulpit and, summoning his people to spiritual inventory, points to the Garden of Eden — which never was — and to Adam and Eve, who never existed — sheer figments of the imagination — for challenge and inspiration! How simpleminded can a Rabbi be?

Nevertheless, please consider my text seriously. It is a

simple one: "Where are you?" In the Hebrew, as given in the Book of Genesis, just one word: *ayeko?*

You remember the legend — a fairy tale, of course. It has inspired and delighted — and misguided, too — millions upon millions of men, women and children in Jewry, Christendom, Islam. The progenitors of *homo sapiens* were enjoying — if they were capable of knowing positive enjoyment — bliss in Paradise: no work, no worry, no taxes, no singing commercials, no traffic jams — and no duties, no dues, not even the common cold; death had not yet seared the minds and bodies of the human race. All they had to do was vegetate — vegetate in eternal bliss. However, one condition was imposed upon them by the Creator: they might not eat the fruit of one tree. You recall the story, which delighted you in your childhood if you were an imaginative child, and which, perhaps, turned you into a child atheist if you were of a skeptical nature. Adam and Eve broke the law. Frightened, they hid themselves. The Voice haunted them: "Where are you?" *ayeko?*

Do not you and I and all the children of Adam and Eve everywhere — and more — do not races and nations and religious communions, and political and economic parties and business enterprises, build Gardens of Eden where they may continue undisturbed by the traffic and demands of the world, resenting and spurning every voice demanding an accounting, desperately resisting any threat to their vested security? Unlike Adam and Eve we are not honest enough to admit: "I am afraid and so I am hiding myself." Instead, we evolve elaborate systems of rationalizations, defending our own little paradises.

Behind our wars are vested injustices. "Wars come upon the world," say our rabbinic masters, "because justice is delayed, and because of them who render wrong decisions."

"Wrong" is a moral term; it has to do with every man's rights and liberties. Wars are "the judgments of the Lord," in the words of the Psalmist, for the injustices of man to man. Abraham Lincoln hurled this truth at his country in the convulsions of the Civil War: "The judgments of the Lord are true and righteous altogether." It was the righteous judgments of the Lord upon a people that had enslaved and exploited other people. Wars do not happen; they are caused, as earthquakes are caused by dislocation of foundations.

Our racial warfare today is the result of centuries of injustice. There is a sliding of foundations. A time has come when the black man will not stay in the place assigned to him by the white man.

Our war on poverty is a crash program because for generations they who have have exploited the have-nots. The privileged have been maintaining themselves in their Gardens of Eden without conscience, without vision, without learning from the history of revolutions. That is the primary cause for the horrors in Africa, Asia.

"Where are you?" Literally, the voice of the Lord is ringing the world over and will not permit the sons and daughters of Adam and Eve to remain slothfully blissful.

I want to direct this question to the personal life.

You and I and all mortals create our own personal Gardens of Eden. We persistently strive to shut out the demands of the world. We do this consciously, more often unconsciously. In the jargon of the day, these are "escapes." *Homo sapiens* is an escape-building, alibi-inventing animal. We build escapes the way birds build nests, quite naturally, unconsciously.

A young man was unburdening himself to me last summer. He was in a tangle of confusion about his college and his marriage. "Have you talked it over with your father?"

I asked him. "No," he said; "my father is away fishing. Every time I want to talk things over with him he is away fishing." To this father I would say this morning, "Where are you?" But he is not here this morning; he is probably away fishing.

Several years ago a young man from one of the graduate schools of our community came to see me about his marriage problem. He was a mature, highly intelligent young man, on the faculty of one of our distinguished universities. I have known his father by reputation — a distinguished Rabbi and scholar. I have read his books and hold him in respect. "Have you talked it over with your father?" I asked him. He looked at me. Obviously he was thinking. "You don't talk such things over with my father. With my father you listen, and that's it."

The first father I mentioned has a hobby, fishing; the second has "convictions." Both are escapes.

Our nursing homes are crowded with aged, sick, disintegrating men and women. Many of them are abandoned. Where are their children?

In many instances a nursing home is the only answer. It would be cruelly wrong and spiritually obtuse to condemn all the children of all the aged people in nursing homes. But many *are* abandoned. It is easier to pay for their keep than to care for them personally. I recall visiting an older woman in one of our hospitals some time ago. She had a magnificent display of flowers in her room. I said something about it. She smiled. Her daughter sends her flowers but will not visit her. She lives in a suburb and it is too difficult — what with transporting the children to school and all that. It is easier to pay the florist than to perform personally — especially when money is not too much of a problem.

Last August a judge in one of our courts castigated forty-one young people and their parents for the rowdyism, vandalism they had perpetrated in one of our neighboring towns. He spoke in solemn indignation: they had brought disgrace upon themselves, their community, their Commonwealth. We agreed with the judge; we appreciated his humanity in not branding these young people with police records for the rest of their lives.

Where were their parents? The parents of the host young man were away on vacation. It is perfectly possible to be at home and away at the same time — on vacation from effective personal responsibility.

I am not pronouncing judgment on all these parents. I know parents — as you do, I am sure — who have been, and constantly are, conscientious and intelligent in the discharge of their duties by their growing children, and who are brokenhearted and crushed by their children's stupidities. Righteous indignation from the pulpit is easy. Too many of us Rabbis are guilty of this. It is easier to denounce than to understand; easier to make sweeping charges and pronounce glittering generalizations than to understand and come up with the right answer. The tragic truth is that scores upon scores of parents — good, intelligent, conscientious — are brokenhearted as they helplessly watch their children makes messes of their lives.

To the young people within the hearing of my voice, on this Rosh Hashanah morning, I address the question: Where are *you,* my young friends — you, brilliant, smart, living on your father's or grandfather's hard earnings for the most part — where are you in your parents' anguish?

The community is calling: hospitals, schools, charities — our own Combined Jewish Appeal, Red Feather — voices of mercy and compassion. Are we hiding ourselves behind our secretaries — "Not in" — or "too busy," or alibis, "Too many appeals," or sophistication, "I don't believe in it"?

Your own synagogue is calling. We are striving to keep faith as a House of God, as a school, as a center whence radiates an influence for righteousness in our community.

I return to my life's emphasis: The Synagogue is the only institution that has saved us Jews these past two thousand years, and the only institution that can save us in our time — when all historic ties are dissolving. It has sheltered us and shielded us in every age: against murderous Crusaders, burning Inquisitors, Nazi beasts. The Synagogue is the only institution that gives meaning to our lives as Jews. We live or die as a people as our synagogues keep faith. There is no ultimate reason for our separate existence as a Jewish people without the heritage the synagogue holds for us.

It takes money to run a synagogue; more, it takes character, and high integrity, and devotion. Your own Temple Sinai is calling. Remember, the men and women who are guiding and guarding your own Temple Sinai are not paid officials. They are doing what they are doing out of sheer devotion. Where are you, where will you be when their appeals for help come?

We return to our Bible story and our text: "Where are you?"

Adam and Eve's first reaction was to hide themselves. The truth to learn from our story is that they were not permitted to remain in hiding.

Neither our fishing, nor our "convictions," nor our "too busy," nor our sophistication, "I don't believe in it," nor any other of our innumerable little paradises will save us against the demands of life and of duty.

Endless are our alibis. We become so habituated to making excuses that we lose the capacity to be responsible.

Perhaps you recall the story of the frog and the hot water. Someone was experimenting with a frog. He dumped it into hot water. It leaped instantly out of the pot. Then he put the frog into cold water; it stayed down. He heated the water a bit; it relaxed and stayed down. He heated the water a little more; it relaxed some more and stayed down. And so, gently, slowly, he heated the water to a boiling point. The frog relaxed, remained at the bottom of the pot and was scalded to death.

Are we so relaxed in our own little private Gardens of Eden that we are disintegrating as morally responsible men and women?

Claude G. Montefiore was one of the founders of liberal Judaism in England — an enormously respected scholar in New Testament and in rabbinics. His name is revered by scholars in Christendom as in Jewry. I quote two sentences from him. He was pleading with his congregation — and he was not a professional Rabbi — to maintain the good name of Jewry in the larger community and to stand true to their Jewish ideals:

> Ten bad Jews may help damn us; ten good Jews may help save us. Which *minyan* will you join?

Yes, which minyan in Temple Sinai will you join? To shift the metaphor, we have a construction crew and a wrecking crew in our own congregation, as there are in every congregation. Where are *you*?

The answer is between yourself and your God.

3

How Tall Are You?
[5727-1966]

SEVERAL weeks ago there was considerable excitement in many of our homes. Children were returning from summer camps. There was the hubbub of reunion — talk, and chatter, and delight, especially in homes where young children were returning — with all their freckles, and blisters, and laundry! Some of our young parents were even astonished: their children were so courteous — a most unusual condition, which lasted a day or two. Amidst the hubbub one special exclamation predominated: "How tall you've grown!" Some mothers stood their children against a wall and measured their heights: an inch, two! Some measured themselves with their children. It is an annual, joyous experience. Thank God.

"How tall you've grown!"

Rosh Hashanah is a good time to ask ourselves, "How tall have *we* grown in the course of the year?" We have lived, we have experienced, we have worked and we have played, in the sunshine and in the shade. Some of us stood with our sons or daughters — or grandchildren — at the marriage altar and heard them speak their marriage vows; some welcomed a new-born; some of us were in beds of illness, or nursed a loved one, and some followed him or her to the final resting place. The young and bright and ambitious among us were admitted to colleges, or received their degrees and entered upon their lives' work; some of us met with business reverses and some scored triumph and success, acquired money and prestige. Yes, all of us go through the valleys of the shadows, and all of us know sunlit stretches on the roads of our lives.

How tall have we grown under these circumstances?

It is the genius of our Days of Awe to rouse introspection and summon us to moral judgment upon ourselves, in full realization of the shadow on the sun dial with its silent warning: "It is later than you think." We therefore return to the primary meaning of our Holy Days, upon which we reflect every year, as we must if we take these sacred days seriously, as our fathers did generation after generation.

Our prayerbook is charged with this moral dynamism. Recall some sentences from our prayers, spoken last night, or this morning, or which we shall rehearse on the Day of Atonement:

> . . . As we grow older in years, we may grow stronger in wisdom, broader in charity, and more steadfast in faith.

Have we?

> Thou who probest the heart and knowest our inmost thoughts, help us to examine ourselves in the light of Thy truth.

> May it [our worship] arouse us to examine all our thoughts and deeds in the light of Thy truth . . .

> O Lord our God, help us to see ourselves as Thou seest us.

I submit that the all-inclusive meaning of our worship is in these sentences, even in this one short sentence: "Help us to see ourselves as Thou seest us." (The petition is inspired by the story in the Book of Samuel. The aged judge, Samuel, was choosing a king to rule over Israel. He had heard of a peasant by the name of Jesse and his sons, in Bethlehem, Judah. He reviews Jesse's sons. His standard was a severe one, and profound: "Look not at his countenance or on the height of his stature; . . . for man judges by outward appearances but the Lord looketh into the heart.")

"As Thou seest us," Thou, from Whom nothing is hid.

This morning, then, on this Day of Remembrance and Day of Judgment, it is not only proper that we reflect on our personal statures; it is our duty.

How tall are you?

The subject is not "we," not "society," not "the nation," and not "the world"; the subject is *I* — every man, every woman, personally; "alone with Thee, my God," as the Psalmist would phrase it.

We can not reform the world, we can not reform our nation, nor our city, nor our family, unless we begin with ourselves. We can not clean up our city by carting off some of the rubble on the streets; we must remove the rubbish from the minds of men, women and children. I have stressed this from our pulpit before and some of you may recall the metaphor I have used: We can not carve rotten wood. We can not build a just, decent world, nor a decent family, nor a righteous city with rotten men and women and children. Resolutions at conferences, impassioned orations or sermons do have value but will not help us much if they do not register in character. Even laws, imperative as they are, will not convert a city — in the words of Isaiah, "a whoring city" — into a righteous, decent city, unless men's hearts and men's minds are cleaned up.

How tall are we, each one of us?

"How tall you've grown!" exclaims the delighted mother, and will stand up her child against some measuring unit, perhaps against herself, back to back. What unit of measurement shall we adopt for ourselves in gauging our own statures?

Many units of measurement suggest themselves; all are conventional, and all are vital: selflessness versus selfishness; generosity versus miserliness, greed; dependability versus irresponsibility; self-reliance versus leaning on some one; maturity (a word which too often is only a puff of wind as used by some) versus adolescent petulance and temper, and self-exhibitionism. In rabbinic lore is a proverb in judging a man's stature; it is a pun: *b'kiso, b'kaaso, b'koso* — a man may be judged by his purse, by his temper, by his cup — that is, how a man manages his money, how he manages his temper, how he controls his drinking. It is as sensible a gauge of a man's character as there is, I presume; but, like all the standards we might list, incomplete and a bit shallow. There are other standards of character not covered by any one I have mentioned.

I should like to pause at four points on the scale of personal stature.

First, money, how we manage our money.

I recall being in a living room some years ago with a number of people, and I recall hearing one of the then prominent women of our community extolling the greatness of a certain person. He was "a great Jew," she proclaimed. As this woman talked, it became clear that all she had to say about this man was that he had money, lots of money. He may have been a great person, for all I knew then; but a great Jew? It is a common belief held in too many quarters.

It is common practice, with quite a number of my colleagues, which has been duly — and justly — satirized, for a Rabbi in the pulpit to take what is supposed to be a "spiritual" stance and look down his nose at money. The opposite is poverty, and poverty is not something we cherish for ourselves nor for our children, nor for our community. Says Tevye in *Fiddler on the Roof*, "being poor is no great honor, either." You recall the Bible report of our ancient ancestors in the brickyards of Egypt. They could not understand Moses when he talked to them of freedom because of their hard labor and depressed spirits. Poverty is a curse. Our nation is making a mighty effort to dispel poverty and the many miseries that breed in its tenements and slums, like rats.

The real question is a double one: How do we manage our money, much or little as we may have; and, what does money do to us? Shrewdly observes Koheleth: "There is a grievous evil which I have seen under the sun, namely, riches kept by the owner to his (own) hurt." Most of us can testify to the truth of this assertion from our own observations. We have seen men and women grow in magnanimity and gain impressive stature with the acquisition of money; and all of us have seen men and women shrink into pigmies when money came into their lives — insufferable egotists and snobs, obnoxiously arrogant. It is sad to observe how, in some people, money only generates more greed, like salt water to a thirsty man.

I submit that we inflict harm on our children by giving them money indiscriminately. If we are to train them in responsibility, in good judgment, we should give them reasonable allowances and insist that they manage their money wisely. We only add to their irresponsibility if we reward them when they come whining for more and more. "With all your getting, get thee understanding," advises the sage in the book of Proverbs.

Money is power, power over our families, over our institutions; thus money is influence. It calls for imagination and for practical wisdom. I feel that too much money may disrupt our families more surely than poverty.

We observe a *second* unit of measurement gauging our personalities: how we manage adversity.

Some of us have known bitter adversity this past year; the cup of bitter wine was put to our lips: illness, bereavement, frustration, disappointment of one sort or another. That is part of the business of living.

How do we manage our adversities? That is a basic unit in determining our statures.

Some collapse, go into a dead faint and add sorrow to their grief, and bring even more sorrow on their loved ones. Some will dash off to the divorce court at the first domestic flareup; others will pause and reflect and look into themselves and draw on their reserves of patience and maturity and strength, and hope for the best. Some, suffering bereavement, will weep and mourn and sink into black depression; others will emerge from the valley and turn the memories of their loved ones into blessings. Schools, hospitals, social centers, sanctuaries of art and sanctuaries of faith are releasing learning, lifting ignorance and pain from the hearts and minds of men and women and children by endowed scholarships, fellowships, chairs, research, laboratories. Some sink into orgies of self-pity, and some go on splurges of one type or another.

Third, how do we behave in the crises of our day? Perhaps it may be an aspect of what we have already observed; but I am thinking more specifically in terms of the social crises of our cities, our country, our world.

We have had a long, hot summer; mobs have gone on rampages. Have you not observed that our cities, the immediate neighborhoods, are promptly victimized by looting? That is the immediate problem for the police or military: the degenerate fringe of our societies that joins the mobs and resorts to looting. The healthy and positive fringes of the community will join the police, or try to help as best they can through the constructive agencies. Most of us bolt our doors and hide. As the crisis gains in violence, the middle group — and I think it is only fair to observe that this means most of us — are not permitted to remain safe in our hiding places. Eventually we must join the lawless or the responsible elements of our society. Which side are we joining?

We have a striking parable of this situation in the ancient story of our ancestors facing the Red Sea. There they were, facing the crisis of their generation, as a community and not merely personally. Before them was the sea; behind them were the armed, enraged hosts of the Pharaoh. The Bible report is vivid. Some cried for returning to the flesh pots of Egypt, the onions and the garlic and the leeks — back to the good old days; some were completely paralyzed with fear and uncertainty. The Voice commands: Forward!

I like to rehearse the old rabbinic story to the effect that the Red Sea did not divide by some magic power; an Israelite jumped into the sea, and when a man — a real man — jumps into the Sea of Trouble, the sea divides and salvation comes.

The children of this generation of the Red Sea came upon their crisis: advancing on or retreating from the Promised Land? Moses had sent out the twelve spies; ten came back with the report: Can't be done! There are giants there! We are only grasshoppers! Two of the twelve dissented: Yes, it can be done. Moses had the genius of following the two, rejecting the preponderant majority. That is what gave Moses his stature as one of the giants in history.

Do we, facing the racial crises of our day, mouth ancient

shibboleths and pious slogans and indirectly line up with the reactionary forces of our time, or are we disenthralling ourselves of wishful thinking, vested emotionalism, and jumping into the Red Sea of our own age? This is a good time in history to recall Lincoln's wise and brave words, spoken when our country was facing the Red Sea of Lincoln's day:

> The occasion is piled high with difficulty and we must rise with the occasion. As our case is new, so we must think anew, act anew. We must disenthrall ourselves, and then we shall save our country.

How tall are we in the racial crisis of our day?

I must specify a *fourth* unit of measurement in determining our statures: how we work with others.

The question penetrates into every area of our lives: husband-wife relationships; parent-children, employer-employee, colleague and friend relationships. Can we work and thrive only when everyone, like the stars in Joseph's dream, bows down to us in adoration? Self-centered, intransigent egotism shrinks a man into a moral pigmy. Intransigent, puny egotism — the Lord deliver us from that. In the old *siddur* is a prayer asking God to deliver us from many trying circumstances. Among these is listed *azoos panim* — impudence, arrogance born of egotism.

Work with some people and you feel tall; work with others and you feel like a worm. How do we work with others? What responses are we arousing in our associates — in business, in our professions, in our organizations, in our congregations?

Last year Mrs. Cohon and I were at the Boston Commons attending a Civil Rights rally. Dr. Martin Luther King was the speaker. Seeing Dr. King on the platform at close range, I observed that he was a shorter man than I had thought. A Negro woman standing by, obviously in modest circumstances, overheard my comment. She replied: "But he makes *you* feel tall!"

How tall do we make others feel?

Lal Bahadur Shastri, the late Prime Minister of India, was five feet two inches in height. Perhaps you recall his likeness: a little man, just over five feet, weighing less than a hundred pounds, toothless, clad in homespun linen, the cap of a commoner on his head. He presided over the destinies of millions upon millions of people and held their confidence and affection. He left an estate, so I recall reading in one newspaper, of some ten dollars in American money. Further, he worked under a man who loomed as a giant, spiritually and physically.

Question: How tall was this little man, five feet two inches?

This morning, then, when we ask God to help us see ourselves as He sees us, let us take a long, clear look into the mirror — on this Day of Remembrance and Day of Judgment. And let us remember that no one looks over our shoulder but God.

4

Are You Listening?
[5731-1970]

ONCE again, my friends, by the grace of God, we are assembled in prayer in response to a call sounded long, long ago. We may not realize it — many of us don't; some may resent, even scorn, the reminder that we are moved by a call spoken centuries upon centuries ago. We are trapped in the tumult and myopia of the NOW generation — NOW, no yesterdays, no tomorrows. NOW is the magic word. NOW! Let the dead past bury its dead. Tomorrow? We will worry about that tomorrow. NOW is all we have, all we know, and all we want to know. That is the frenzy of our time. Ultimately it means no vision, no horizons, no perspective!

But, here we are this Rosh Hashanah morning, gathered in prayer — reluctantly, perhaps, some of us; out of the habit of the years, perhaps out of undefined uneasiness, others of us. We do hear the rumblings of distant drums on the horizon of our lives. Fall is here; the leaves are turning and falling about us. The chill of autumn is in the air. The shofar does sound and awakens echoes within us. Perhaps as long as four thousand years ago was the proclamation made:

> And the Lord spoke unto Moses, saying: Speak unto the children of Israel, saying: In the seventh month, in the first day of the month, shall be a solemn rest unto you, a memo-

rial proclaimed with the blast of the shofar, a holy convocation. (Lev. 23.23)

And here we are, in the year 5731, in obedience to the ancient command.

Hearing the call across the centuries and responding is the meaning of this Day of Remembrance. We are loyal to the covenant by which we have been sustained as a people all these centuries upon centuries.

Whatever our slogans and clichés, a calendar does govern our lives; a biologic clock, if nothing more, does control the days of our years. A schedule, a beginning and a progression, from stage to stage, moves on inexorably, and who shall say: "What doest Thou?" There are springs and summers, and autumns, and the leaves turn and are scattered by the winds, and when winter comes, as it must, will there be another spring for us, personally, in the land of the living? It registers in our faces and in our bones, and no art of the beautician can arrest it — conceal it for a while, yes, but stop it, no! To realize this fully and accept it, emotionally as well as intellectually, not merely routinely, is the business of living, if we are to have a measure of wisdom in our lives.

This morning, to help focus on the central meaning of Rosh Hashanah, I raise the questions: Are you listening? Am I listening? Are you and I listening — listening to whom, and listening to what?

First, I would stress the imperative need to develop the *capacity* to listen, to listen intently, sincerely, sincerely trying to understand, patiently, intelligently listening to each other, and trying to hear what the rolling waves of the years are saying to us personally.

Many of us do not have the mental discipline to listen. We are too absorbed with ourselves, with our personal aches and hurts, real or imaginary, and too absorbed with our personal petty ambitions and smart schemes. Scatter-brained people, self-centered people, do not hear what the person talking to them is saying. Their attention is on the next one in line, the more important one. Have not all of us had this experience at one time or another, especially at social splurges when the drinks are on the house? We do not listen; we only tolerate another speaking. At the first break in the verbal traffic we dash — back to ourselves, as if nothing had been said by the person speaking.

And, more, if we listen at all we listen only to what we like to hear, only what is pleasing and flattering to us. We simply do not hear what is unpleasant. Still more: Certain words, phrases, labels "turn us off" altogether. We have our escape mechanisms and we work them unconsciously. Labels such as "Communist," "Fascist," "Radical," "Racist," or the name of a political figure of whom we disapprove, or clichés — "Law and Order," "Black Power," for example — and we unconsciously "pull the plug." We hear no more; all we hear is sound.

Would we be effective parents, effective teachers, preachers, friends, effective members of working committees or governing boards? We must learn to listen, listen patiently, listen creatively (perhaps even painfully), listen to all with whom we associate in sincerity.

Young people complain, "Nobody is listening! Nobody pays any attention to us." Much truth — and much sorrow — are in this complaint.

We hear it everywhere. Homes are tense; campuses are battlefields. Everybody is shouting slogans. Who is listening to whom? Where we do have a decent effort at listening — in the cliché of our day, "a line of communication" — the situation is at least partially under control.

Recently, a friend reported that he had been invited to

Parents' Day at his daughter's college. The invitation was to listen to the young people present their views. He was deeply disturbed. Shall he go to listen to the young people? Should not the young people be willing to listen to him, too, in turn? The young people clamor for "dialogue." Dialogue means a give-and-take. Only tragedy results when we dismiss in contempt what the young are saying. The Heard Report to the President on campus disturbances asserts: "Students may seem baffling and chaotic to some, but they have a deep moral commitment to eliminate the ills of American Society . . . Given the integrity, idealism and passion of the students, the Administration would be well advised to listen to them." Granted; of course. But should not these very students listen in turn? Is all wisdom, all truth, locked up in their young heads? Fantastic arrogance!

Listening is an attempt at understanding. It is easier to condemn than to understand. I return to the text by which I have tried to live all my life, and by which I have striven to guide this congregation, and which is inscribed over the ark of our synagogue, "Grant me understanding that I may live."

And how many homes, and how many marriages, and how many friendships would be saved if parents and children, husbands and wives, offended friends, listened to each other — not merely stopped talking (though that would help a great deal), but listened sympathetically, sincerely, listened not the way the prosecutor listens — intent on spotting a hole in the argument so that he may pounce — but listened (shall I say?) "with a little bit of love"? It is not easy, of course, especially when we enjoy our own eloquence, our own self-righteousness, or when we are convinced that the person speaking does not know what he is talking about. Yes, it is a sore trial to listen to endless talk with neither facts nor logic detectable. But that is the test of maturity and love in dealing with all who are dear to us.

Second, the other side of the shield.

If we want our husbands, our wives, our children, our students, our associates to listen to us, we must have their confidence. We must earn their respect first. Respectful attention can not be had on demand. Nobody listens to anyone he considers a phony. We "turn them off," as we should, quickly. Life is too short.

Parents shouting at their children, husbands and wives snapping at each other, teachers, preachers nagging, haranguing, only produce irritating noise on our ear drums. Writing his laborious essays in rural Concord, a century and a half ago, Ralph Waldo Emerson noted a basic truth. He wrote: "I can not hear what you are saying; your actions thunder in my ears." *What* we are drowns out what we say.

I recall an incident.

Walking down the street in the neighborhood of our Temple some time ago, I observed a car pulling up to the curb. A father and his young son were in the front seat. I heard the boy say, "Dad, we can't park here. Here is a sign, "NO PARKING, police take notice." And I heard the father say, "Ah, forget it! I can fix it."

The son by now may be at college involved in the youth disturbances of our day, and the father may harangue him about law and order and respecting the police. He lost his son's respect a long time ago and has forfeited his influence. The "image" is a terrible reality. The image the son has of his father jams the son's reception.

The bleary-eyed father and mother, hell-bent on enjoying themselves at all costs, may harangue their children about the evils of alcohol or drugs. All the children hear is noise. No conviction comes through. What we *are,* not what we *say,* carries conviction.

I submit this, most respectfully, for your mature consideration.

And please bear in mind: I am not urging this as the complete solution of our problem. I can name instances, as you can, where everything was done right, "according to the book," but everything came out all wrong. I know of exemplary parents, as you do, who are brokenhearted. But I am offering it as a basic factor, a major consideration for every mature man and woman to contemplate earnestly.

First, are we listening patiently, sincerely, intelligently? *Second,* are our beloved ones, our associates, listening to us? If not, why not? *Third,* are we listening to ourselves? Do we hear, do we heed the still small voice above the din and clatter and clichés of our day, in some precious still hour?

Most of us are afraid of silence. And no wonder. Roaring traffic, planes overhead, screaming bulletins on the radio or television, bombings, burnings, killings, riots; Vietnam, the Middle East; college campuses, ghettos, race riots. We retire with the radios or TVs, the idiotic forced laughter of the comedians ringing in our ears. As soon as our eyes are open, we snap on the radios; again, violence, bombings, killings, rioting, more singing commercials.

I call on a house of mourning, in the awesome shadow of death, and I can't get out fast enough: talk, talk, chatter, and food and drinks and more food and more drinks. Where is reverence for the dead, at least for the awesome reality of death? Back in the sixteenth century, Joseph Caro codified long-established customs associated with death and mourning in Jewish practice. He specifies how friends calling on a house of mourning should behave. The caller sits down quietly by the side of the bereaved and is silent, taking his cue from the mourner. Only when the mourner breaks the silence may he speak. Silence, the quiet presence of a friend, brings comfort. "There is a time to speak and a time to keep silent."

Even our prayers are noisy. I recall asking the children of the Confirmation Class some years ago which of the Sabbath morning prayers in our prayerbook they preferred. Several selected the silent devotion as their favorite.

I have stressed the need to develop our capacities to listen to others. I am now stressing the importance of listening to ourselves, listening to the still small voice from the silent recesses of our hearts and minds.

To some voices welling up from within we do listen. These may be the songs of the Lorelei, luring us to the rocks of destruction: resentment, anger, revenge.

Remember Captain Ahab in Melville's *Moby Dick*? He heard the call to revenge on the white whale; he was possessed by maniacal anger, chasing the white beast over the infinite ocean. He could hear nothing else in his life. He had been hurt, he lost a leg, and he was bitter, enraged, consumed by a passion for revenge. Nothing else could penetrate his soul. Revenge. Bitterness, bitterness toward God and man.

Grudges, peeves, hurts, insults — real and imaginary, mainly imaginary — haunt some of us throughout the years — against all reason, and pervert our thinking and twist our personalities.

I have recalled Captain Ahab and *Moby Dick*. I recall another personality, not as famous, who too listened and was overcome.

On a Sunday morning in the winter of the year 1697, Judge Samuel Sewall, of our own Bay State, stopped his minister on the way to Church and handed him a communication. He asked the minister to read it from the pulpit. The minister read the note, while Judge Sewall stood, alone of the congregation, all eyes focused on him. The Judge confessed to God and to the congregation that a sentence of guilty, in which he had concurred with other judges, convicting someone of witchcraft, was wrong. He had brooded over the sentence, searched his reason and his conscience; he had erred, he was wrong. On a Sabbath morning, in the presence of God and his friends and fellow worshippers, he stood up and confessed and begged forgiveness.

Judge Sewall too was haunted by a voice.

Do you say it was a most extraordinary case, in a religiously-oriented society? Yes. But voices still speak to all of us if we but listen.

The Black Panthers do listen and are possessed by maniacal fury, as Captain Ahab was. They are possessed by the voices of revenge, resentment of a horrible history, self-righteous martyrdom. They hear nothing else; the voices of reason, good judgment, faith in their friends and faith in schools, courts of justice, their government are silenced. The voices of rage and violence are all they hear. Bombing, burning, killing — blind Samsons bringing down the Temple of Civilization.

Of Superintendent of Schools of Williamsburg County, South Carolina, a Mr. Fennell, it was reported several months ago that he had initiated a study of the reading capacities of the children in his schools. The survey disclosed that one out of three children in the seventh grade was a nonreader. Mr. Fennell is reported as saying, "They are my product. All those black children started in the first grade while I was superintendent and I am responsible for their disabilities."

To which voices do we listen? Which do we silence? Rosh Hashanah is designated in our tradition as a Day of Remembrance. We recall; we remember. I wish we developed, more specifically, by way of completing the spiritual message of the day, the need to forget, the importance of washing our minds clean of soiled memories that pervert our personalities.

Would we cultivate mental health? Would we develop refreshing reservoirs within ourselves? That is part of the urgent business of the High Holy Days.

Would we create, those of us who strive to write, or paint, or teach creatively, or achieve artistry in our lives and inspire artistry in the lives of our dear ones? Listen.

Irving Stone in his great novel, *The Agony and the Ecstasy*, depicts Michelangelo in his early life. He writes:

> Michelangelo pulled back into his seat and sat with his head resting on the back of the chair . . . He listened to his own voice. One thing he knew for certain: his first theme could not come from Athens or Cairo or Rome or even Florence. It had to come from him, something he knew and felt and understood. Otherwise he would be lost. A work of art was not like a work of scholarship; it was personal, subjective. It had to be born within.

God grant all of us a good, creative year. May He refresh the reservoirs of our lives.

5

When the Foundations Are Destroyed, What Can the Righteous Do?
[5730-1969]

IT is amazing how a question raised some three thousand years ago, phrased in archaic Hebrew, strikes at the heart of our personal and social problems, like an arrow shot by an expert archer hitting the bull's-eye. We find it imbedded in Psalm Eleven. Our own Jewish Publication Bible renders it, "When the foundations are destroyed, what hath the righteous wrought?" (11.3). The Elizabethan English blunts its point even more than the archaic Hebrew. The Oxford Annotated Bible gives it a sharper translation:

> If the foundations are destroyed,
> what can the righteous do?

Evidently the ancient is thinking of the social structure of his day as a building with rotting, collapsing foundations. He feels himself trapped. What can he, an innocent, lone person do? He believes himself to be a decent, righteous man. He employs the word *tsadik,* which has been corrupted in our time by the *hasidim;* they mean by it a miracle-working pietist, a healer. All it means in the Bible is a just, honorable, God-fearing man. What can a just, honorable, God-fearing man do when everything about him is sagging because the foundations are rotting and crumbling?

You see what a vital question the ancient is raising, and

how pertinent it is in our own time, for all of us who would be honorable, decent, God-fearing men and women — as parents, as teachers, as doctors, lawyers, rabbis, as citizens, as directors of businesses and institutions. You see how pertinent it is for us especially on Rosh Hashanah, when we are enjoined by our tradition to search our hearts and minds as responsible Jews.

This morning is the thirty-first Rosh Hashanah that I am privileged — by the grace of God and your sufferance — to speak from the Sinai pulpit. Always, every year, have I recalled the Hebrew phrase *heshban hanafesh,* personal, spiritual inventory, personal stocktaking. Unless we do search our own hearts and minds and pronounce honest judgment upon ourselves — not merely on everyone else, not merely upon the nations and the races — our presence here this morning, rehearsing our prayers, is only going through the paces of conventional routine. It is easy to condemn the nations and the races; it is not easy to condemn ourselves in the secret places of our own hearts and minds. That is why I am addressing myself this morning, and am inviting you to consider with me, the psalmist's question:

> If the foundations are destroyed,
> What can the (lone) righteous man do?

It compels self-examination, and that is the burden of this day.

We know nothing of the man who phrased this verse originally. This morning is not the time to involve ourselves in academic textual analysis. But it may help us grasp the relevance of this question if we note its setting.

We note, first, as we read this psalm, that the man speaking is under severe pressure. He is menaced. We note, second, that friends urge him to flee for safety. Reference is made to a bird, and "flee to the mountains." We note, third, that he rejects the advice. There is no safety in flight. He must stand true to his faith in his God and meet whatever it is that menaces him.

It is amazing, I say, how the ancient, once his thought is extricated from archaic verbiage, shoots his arrow straight into our hearts.

Are there any among us who will not concede that the strains and disruptions that menace our homes, our families, our schools, our cities are only surface manifestations of deep decadence at the foundations? Our generation gap, our campus riots, our race warfare, our sex revolution (and alley-cat morality), unseemly vulgarity polluting our literature, our theatre, our sanctuaries of art and religion no less, issue from degeneration deep in our personal and social lives. In these vast upheavals, what can those of us who consider ourselves — or who would be — honorable, decent, God-fearing men and women, do to preserve a measure of personal integrity, at least a residue of personal refinement? What can we do as parents, as teachers, as social workers, as rabbis, as citizens? Can we walk with crowds and keep our virtue?

Consider what is happening all around us, and let us try to judge from the standpoint of the sacred the High Holy Days represent.

Our cities are deep in garbage; avalanches of garbage are threatening to bury us. Garbage everywhere. Smog everywhere. Chimneys, cars, airplanes are belching exhaust all around us, all over us. Our air, our lakes and streams, our rivers are polluted. Our lungs are black with soot. There is no refuge for anyone, anywhere. Fish and fowl are poisoned. We are facing a terribly grim challenge.

Even so it is with our intellectual, moral lives. Garbage everywhere; torrents of sex-depravity are inundating us. Our minds, like our lungs, are black with soot.

Recently I came on a penetrating essay by an author of insight and taste.* She addresses herself to her literary colleagues who still hold on to "the intolerable burden of standards." She alerts them to the all-pervasive rot in our popular novels. All one needs, she writes, is relevance, by which is meant, invariably, open, brashy pornography. "Life has no meaning, so why should a book have any? Order is a lie, anarchy is truth. Stop looking in books for something that will either clarify, illumine or exalt. The writer doesn't owe you anything but himself, and if he happens to be revolting, that's your tough luck and the public's delight . . . You must applaud this new freedom and constantly remind yourself (as you drown in the polluted verbal stream) that life is a sewer . . . Fornication is freedom . . . Stop looking for nice people in books; kind, intelligent, brave, loyal and loving. You may find a few, but they will probably be cripples or retarded and therefore tragic (which is okay). It's much more fun to be a . . . . [Here I cannot bring myself to use a word from the pulpit. But my dictionary defines it as a wingless insect feeding on the bodies of men and animals.] It makes for a new kind of brotherhood. . . . If you come across a book with cultivated, witty and well-mannered people, give it hell. It's irrelevant to our times — which is indeed, if lamentable, true. Just be content to stuff yourself with sex, relentlessly explicit and supremely trivial."

The same, of course, is true of the theatre, the television: psychotic killings and sex maniacs pouring into our living

---

* Marya Mannes, N.Y. Times Book Review, April 27, 1969.

rooms and bedrooms. We need not know anything, not even how to read; all we need is the capacity to sit and stare. Rock music draws hundreds of thousands — three hundred thousand to one performance in upper New York recently — maladjusted, aimless young people, adventurous innocents, psychotics, dope victims, dropouts from school and from life, according to its sponsors. We are promised more next year. The central issue of the theatre at the moment seems to be nudity. (Incidentally, what shall I say to your sons or daughters when they say to me, "God is dead; religion is obsolete."?)

We Jews have a special affliction in our sophisticated emancipation: the so-called "Jewish novel." Our popular Jewish novelists are in a historic procession of noble writers of integrity and vision: Isaiah, Jeremiah in ancient times; Yehuda Halevi in Medieval ages; in our own time: Zangvill, Heine, Wasserman, the Zweigs; Bialik and Agnon in our own day — to snatch a few names at random. But many of our popular Jewish writers today represent a tragic betrayal of the most precious heritage cherished by the People of the Book. And why not? Did Isaiah ever receive the wealth our pornographers are collecting?

Of course there are fine and great books — fine and great plays, poems — published in our day. Thank God. But we need discernment to choose the good and reject the evil. Discernment, insight, independent judgment, the capacity to withstand the gusts of vulgarity.

Which brings us back to the Psalmist and his desperate question. What can the lone individual do at such a time?

This morning I wish to urge two major considerations to help us meet the challenge, one from the realm of social action and one from the sphere of the personal and spiritual. Time will not permit a fuller consideration.

First, the lone, obscure individual can do, and does do, a great deal, and can do much more. Reflect on several examples.

On a day in December, 1955, a woman by the name of Rosa Parks, a seamstress, dropped her fare in the box as she boarded a bus in Montgomery, Alabama, and took the first seat she came upon. The conductor asked her to move to the Jim Crow section. She was black. She refused. She was tired; her feet were tired, and her soul was tired of the segregation indecency. She refused to pay the penalty prescribed by segregationist law. You recall the story. The Civil Rights rebellion flared up. A bus strike; national rebellion; Doctor Martin Luther King assumed leadership. The Montgomery buses were desegregated. The humble, black seamstress, with her tired feet, and her tired soul refreshed, and countless thousands of her black sisters and brothers, are riding the buses in dignity. One poor, tired seamstress in a Montgomery ghetto. What can the individual do?

I take the liberty of citing two examples, involving two members of our own congregation. One of them is here this morning, I assume; the other has gone to his eternal rest.

Ralph Sussman, of blessed memory, was not a wealthy man; he had no battery of lawyers, no public-relations men, no lobbyists at the State House. But he had a conviction and a will. There should be comfortable apartments for the elderly in our community at reasonable rental rates. Highrise apartments have gone up all around us; most of them replaced humbler dwellings and crowded out aged people of modest means. He took it upon himself to agitate for apartments for the elderly here in Brookline. Real estate men were against him, and they did have lawyers and lobbyists. Mr. Sussman kept at it. He talked to the Selectmen, he talked to the city authorities, he was in and out of the Town Hall, over and over again. Many, I am sure, considered him a pest. I had the privilege of participating in the exercises dedicating a room to Ralph and his beloved Fannie Sussman in a new apartment house for the elderly on Marion Street, around the corner from our Temple. And when you walk down Pleasant Street, two or three blocks from Temple Sinai, you note a lovely new apartment house for the elderly bearing the name of Ralph Sussman. One man with imagination and a will!

Consider another example. If you walk down St. Paul Street, from Beacon towards Commonwealth Avenue, you come on a lovely little park, only a block long, next to a playground for little children. It was recreated in response to the imagination and will of one of our cherished members. This brave woman decided that the neglected spot should have flowers, hedges, benches where tired folk might rest in the heat of the day. I find myself walking in that direction as I perambulate in our neighborhood. One woman, and no budget, no noisy protests, no publicity agents. Imagination; determination.

What can an obscure individual do? "Go fight City Hall"?

The individual has a number of tools at hand. He can write letters, for one. Thank God we are living in an open society and we have the right to petition and to protest. The Constitution of the United States legislates, "Congress shall make no law . . . abridging the right of the people . . . to petition the government for redress of grievances."

One hundred thousand pieces of mail reach the Capitol daily. That's a powerful force in saving our democracy. Do you resent the filth that is pouring into our homes over the television? Write to the manager of the station. Do you resent the killings and the muggings? Do you resent the pollution all around us, physical, spiritual? Write to your newspaper; write to your President, the Senator, the Congressman, the Board of Selectmen. A letter from the humble citizen is effective. Many a bill in Congress carries or dies still-born depending upon the volume of mail that reaches the legislators.

Most of us belong to organizations — civic, fraternal, cultural, social, religious; we belong to luncheon clubs, congregations, Sisterhoods, Brotherhoods, Parent-Teachers groups. Write and get your fellow members to write. Or, are we satisfied to belong and remain zeros? Be a figure of consequence. Stand up, speak up, in open meeting or by mail, and be counted. It is astonishing how powerful the humble individual can be if he bestirs himself.

The lawyers here this morning will recall the name of Clarence Gideon. He was a shiftless character in Florida, in and out of jail most of his life. One day he was arrested on the charge of robbing a poolroom. He was tried and sent to jail. In jail he scribbled a note, on jail stationery, to the United States Supreme Court, complaining that he had not been defended by counsel. He couldn't afford a lawyer. The Supreme Court provided him with legal counsel, granted him a new trial, and exonerated him. More, the Supreme Court voted that every man has the right to have counsel provided for him if he is financially unable to engage a lawyer for himself. A major extension of American justice effected by an obscure man in jail, with one letter.

What can an obscure individual do? One man with imagination and a will — and, of course, a just cause — can do, does do, great things. He is saving our democracy and the integrity of our institutions. Imagination and will! We used to call it "character." Remember? Character. Have you heard the word lately? We used to talk of "character education" for our children. Remember?

Dead fish float with the stream; live fish swim against it.

Second, from the personal, the spiritual.

We can turn off the psychotic killers, the sex maniacs, the degenerates on our TV sets; we can boycott the ill-smelling novel. But for that we need discernment and will. For that we must shake ourselves loose from the cheap, sell-out philosophy, "Everybody is doing it; everybody is reading it; we must be in step with the times."

The songs of the Lorelei are luring us to degeneration. We follow the crowd in the name of relevance and modernity and popularity; we have not the backbones to step out of line and speak up for ourselves. And so we are drowning in mediocrity.

We are mesmerized by words — noble words in themselves, corrupted in popular usage. I have time to cite only several from a long list.

We greet each other on our Days of Awe with the noble term, *l'shanah tova,* and then, unconsciously, we yield to the pagan corruption of our time and translate it, *"Happy New Year." L'shanah tovah* does not mean a *happy* new year; that is paganism that has rotted our synagogues and our religious life. It even got into our prayerbook! What it does mean is, a *good* year, and what is good is much more important than what merely makes us happy. It isn't important that we be happy; it is important that we be good, just, truthful, compassionate, decent, responsible.

"Love" is a noble word, of course; but it is corrupted tragically, and may — and unfortunately does only too often — express only promiscuity and degeneration. A redeeming word degenerates into alley-cat morality.

"Self-fulfillment" is another tragic corruption. It may mean only self-indulgence. It depends on who uses the word. And, like happiness, we want our self-fulfillment now, now, immediately, spontaneously. No yesterdays and no tomorrows, no planting and no harvesting, no personal effort, no self-sacrifice of any sort. Now, instantaneously! "Fly now and pay later," if we must pay at all.

"Realism" and "relevance" are cited by our novelists to justify their reveling in degeneracy. Even educators, secular and religious too, are mouthing "relevance." "Keep the kids happy."

Again, these are noble words; in practice they may mean only pitiless mediocrity, only decadence. A garbage can is real; but is not an orchid real? Psychotic killers, sex perverts are real; are not self-sacrificing fathers or mothers or teachers or doctors, real? And just what does "relevance" mean in our religious education? How relevant is the Twenty-third Psalm? the *sh'ma?* the *kaddish, kiddush?* the *kol nidre?* the *Sabbath?*

Is it not the business of our Jewish educators, particularly in our religious schools, to *make* these basic terms and concepts of our faith relevant?

We entered on our worship last night, as we did last year, as our fathers have done generation after generation back to the dim dawn of our history, with the lofty affirmation of the Psalmist: "I lift mine eyes unto the mountains . . . ."; with the prophet we have prayed: "Ho, everyone that thirsteth come ye to the waters . . .", the living waters of faith and hope and dedication to all that is just and good. We sounded the Shofar, summoning the responsible Jew to remembrance, to judgment, to alert him to divine sovereignty. With the liturgist we have prayed, "Enable us to see ourselves as Thou seest us." The mighty affirmation of our faith is behind these texts: we are partners with the Holy One in shaping our world and our personal lives.

We have work to do, you and I: loads to lift, ugliness, ignorance to dispel, wrongs to right, visions to maintain in eternal focus of God's will. God alone makes a swamp; God and man make a garden.

For that we need dedication and will and personal integrity, character.

I covet for the Synagogue — and for our own Temple Sinai particularly, since it is our synagogue — devotion to this supreme task: clearing our vision as Jews, stiffening our backbones as positive Jews and personalities of refinement. Ultimately that is about all that justifies our existence as Jews in a free, open American democracy.

I pray that all of you may be blessed with a good year, with life and health and achievement, and peace — peace in your hearts, and peace in your homes.

6

Let Not Arrogance Come Out of Your Mouth
[5729-1968]

RECALL with me, my friends, a scene from an ancient drama — I should say, an ancient *tragedy*. It holds up a light to us, and light we need desperately, trapped as we are in a maze of caves haunted by demons: the demons of race hatred, violence on our streets, roving gangs of our own children in defiance of every civilizing restraint, the rolling drums of propaganda in an election year, screaming obscenity pouring into our homes. It is a scene familiar to most of you, I hope, from your Religious School days.

In the foreground is a depressed woman at an altar, lost in reverie, pouring out her soul in prayer; in the background, on a bench, "beside the doorpost of the temple of the Lord," is an aged priest observing her. You recognize Hannah and Eli at Shiloh. We read Hannah's Song of Faith as the *haftarah* for this Rosh Hashanah morning:

> My heart exults in the Lord . . .
> Talk no more so very proudly,
>   let not arrogance come out of your mouth;
> For the Lord is a God of knowledge,
>   by Him actions are weighed. . . .

She had come to the sanctuary in the grip of bitter frustration. She was childless. Childlessness is always a cruel frustration to women who want children. In Bible

ARROGANCE

times childlessness was a badge of shame; it was considered punishment administered by God. For Hannah it was an even more stinging pain; her rival wife — a perfectly legitimate institution in those days — did have children. Peninah was cruel; she taunted Hannah. Thus, at the altar, we see the unhappy Hannah pouring out her soul in prayer. The Bible passage is haunting: "She was deeply distressed and prayed unto the Lord, and wept bitterly." The old priest observes her at some distance. Again Bible speech is more moving than our prosaic paraphrasing:

> Hannah was speaking in her heart; only her lips moved, and her voice was not heard; therefore Eli took her to be a drunken woman. And Eli said to her, "How long will you be drunken? Put away your wine from you." But Hannah answered, "No, my lord, I am a woman sorely troubled; I have drunk neither wine nor strong drink, but I have been pouring out my soul before the Lord. Do not regard your maidservant as a base woman, for all along I have been speaking out of my great anxiety and vexation. (I Sam. 1.12–16)

Eli was not an evil man; he did not mean to hurt poor Hannah. On his own level he was, no doubt, a good and upright man, revered by his people. His intentions were of the best; but he had no insight, no perception, no sympathetic understanding.

You and I, my friends, have lived long enough to learn what grievous evils are perpetrated by "good and upright men." It is appalling to contemplate. Families, homes, schools, governments, institutions of every type are corrupted by conventionally good men with highest motives; they simply lack understanding of what they are saying and doing.

Besides, Eli — like so many good men — was weighed down with personal problems. He had presided a lifetime over the sanctuary at Shiloh; his two sons were succeeding him. But they were corrupt men. The Bible brands them in contempt as *b'nei b'liyaal*: "base men who knew not the Lord." We would say, "racketeers." Their chief concern was, in the language of our day, "fringe benefits." And they had quite a racket going their way. The old priest's heart was as heavy as Hannah's.

There he is: looking but not seeing, observing but not perceiving. Hannah's answer must have stung him; the kindly spirit awoke in the aged, heavy-laden priest. His response is one of the most tender sentences in the Bible:

> Go in peace, and the God of Israel grant your petition which you have made of him.

Several months ago I was at the Harvard Divinity School and found myself reading material on the bulletin board while waiting for my appointment. On the board before me was a column of a newspaper reporting an address the newly-appointed Dean, Dr. Krister Stendahl, had delivered to his students. He urged the future ministers to remember that if they were to speak from their pulpits helpfully they must know what is in the hearts of the people in the pews.

If you and I are men and women of discernment, responsible citizens, responsible parents, responsible teachers, true to the professions we are voicing, we must make an honest effort to silence the clamor, the shouting of brutal slogans, the oratory of brash men, and try to understand what is in the hearts of men and women all around us; yes, what is in our own hearts and minds and in the hearts and in the minds of our rebellious youth. Remember the warning that came to the overzealous, self-righteous prophet, Elijah: *lo boraash adonoy,* the Lord is not in the whirlwind. Let us turn off our radios, our television sets, put away our newspapers and our placards and listen for a while — listen to the still small voice within ourselves. Remember: there is nothing more dreadful than rampaging self-righteousness born of ignorance.

I wish to direct our reflections this morning and apply this truth to the desperate need for understanding in one area of our life as a nation especially. Time will not permit further exploration.

Racism.

We so-called white Americans, of whatever religious communion or cultural grouping, have been branded "racists" — all of us, whatever our official religious pronouncements, whatever our political party platform. The indictment is made by honest men who have searched our life as a nation most conscientiously, most competently. In the language of our prayers for these Sacred Days all of us must say, "Yea, we have sinned, we have transgressed, we have done perversely." The civil war in our streets, the burning and the looting, bring to mind the words of the Psalmist: "The judgments of the Lord are true and righteous altogether." Lincoln was haunted by these words while the flames of the Civil War raged about him.

Last winter we read of an incident at a White House reception given by the wife of the President to a group of distinguished women active in the cultural-social life of the nation: social workers, teachers, writers, artists. We read of an emotional explosion on the part of a Negro singer, Eartha Kitt. Turning on her hostess she shouted, "I have to say what is in my heart. I have lived in the gutters." Hot, enraged words came tumbling from her mouth. Some of us may have thought — some of you said so in my hearing — that she was rude; a social gathering at the White House is no place for such outbursts by an invited guest. Perhaps so. The Prophet Nathan was equally rude when he pointed his finger at King David in the royal palace and flung into his teeth words that have come ringing down the ages: "Thou art the man!"

Mrs. Johnson, of course, is not personally responsible for all the evils that afflict the black community. I am recalling the incident because of the truth embodied in Mrs. Johnson's reply. Said the First Lady to Miss Kitt: "I am sorry. I can not understand the things that you do. I have not lived with the background that you have."

Here is the gulf that must be bridged. We in our separate and separatistic camps can not understand what is in the hearts and minds of the people in opposing camps. We Jews should understand that. We were in Egypt — in many Egypts; we should know the heart of the dispossessed.

Recently I received a booklet from VISTA. It has some superb photographs. One of these is that of a little Negro girl — say, ten years old — her chin in the palms of her hands, looking straight at you — an attractive, intelligent child. Under the picture are lines she is supposed to speak. "My idea of beauty is a straight nose, thin lips, blond hair, white skin. *My* nose is flat, *my* lips are heavy, *my* hair is kinky, and I am black all over; I hate myself!"

Can our overprivileged children, with all the goodwill in the world, understand this child? Can you and I with all our courses and degrees in psychology and communication? All the placards, all the marching, all the shouting of slogans, all the statistics of the sociologists will not save this little black girl from growing into an embittered, frustrated, angry woman, especially in a hostile environment where she will be rebuffed at every turn. Multiply this a millionfold and we begin to see the enormity of our racial problem. Slums may be cleared; employment may be found; disease, drunkenness may be mitigated in some measure; schools may be improved; but the depths of our racial misery are not reached.

ARROGANCE 55

My friends, I am trying to grasp, and encourage you to grasp, a fleeting view of the enormity of the plague that is ravaging our country and the world.

There are further dimensions to the complexity of our racial problem; I have time to concentrate on one: *black racism*.

I am not thinking of the riots, the arson, the looting that ravage our cities. Speaking from a synagogue pulpit on Rosh Hashanah, I am concerned especially with the malicious spirit that has gripped so many of the talented, highly-gifted black artists, novelists, playwrights, teachers, performers — the choice black men and women who might be — who should be — the teachers and guides and redeemer of the black people. The same evil racism that possesses white people possesses them, even more inflamed, the same vicious anti-Semitism, even the same slogans that were hurled by Hitler and his evil brood. The Negro novel, play, lecture platform, belch race hatred and rouse insane burning and looting and sniping. Tragic — tragic beyond words!

Consider one or two examples.

Some of us have read — or are reading now — William Styron's novel, "The Confessions of Nat Turner." The book depicts a Negro revolt in Virginia before the Civil War. Mr. Styron utilizes what skimpy information we have of Nat Turner. He has earned a fine reputation as a novelist. His latest work is not the greatest novel of the age, but it is an honest, solid piece of work. Mr. Styron is strongly sympathetic to the Negro cause, and is appreciative of the paradoxical nature of the would-be black liberator and martyr.

Recently appeared a book of essays by ten Negro authors purporting to answer Mr. Styron. A distinguished historian has sadly branded this so-called answer as an *assault* on the author. Vile names are heaped on the author by these essayists because he does not glorify the hero as the black romanticists would have him. He is branded as "an unreconstructed Southern racist."

It is not only sad; it is tragic. Literary criticism gives way to racial polemics; the same racial chauvinism that degrades the writing of the white racists is poisoning the writings of the black racists.

In our own city Negro leaders are demanding that only Negro principals be engaged for schools in black neighborhoods. Emphasis is not on competence, not on excellence; emphasis is on color, race. At the same time white parents in Mississippi are in rebellion against the local school authorities because they appointed four black teachers to their white school. What is the difference? And why not black judges only for black neighborhoods, and white judges only for white neighborhoods — and Chinese, Japanese, Mexican, Puerto Rican teachers and judges for Chinese, Japanese, Mexican, Puerto Rican neighborhoods? And ultimately why not a negro governor for the negro citizens and a white governor for the whites, and why not carry the nightmare still further: a Presidium of several Presidents of the United States representing all racial strains of America? That is an omen of catastrophe not only for our country but for our world. We Jews would be doomed to toleration as a racial minority as our parents and grandparents were in Poland. The Lord of mercy deliver us!

We must disenthrall ourselves of our own clichés, our slogans, our campaign oratory — drop our placards and try to understand in depth. This calls for integrity of thought and backbone. We are in the grip of a new tyranny: slogans, catchwords, placards!

We must remember, at the peril of our souls and at the

peril of our nation, that there is nothing as horrifying as ignorance on the rampage in selfrighteousness.

If there is such an evil as "original sin," it is racism mated with xenophobia, nursed by self-righteousness.

We hear campaign orators shouting "law and order." Of course law and order. Is there a sane man who is opposed to that? But there is law and order in Prague today — established by orderly rows of Russian tanks. There was law and order of sorts in the concentration camps. Our rabbinic masters have given us the formula for salvation in this matter: "The world is sustained by three forces: justice, truth and peace." First are justice and truth; peace is the result of justice and truth, not the result of tanks.

We have recalled the story of Hannah and Eli at Shiloh and tried to grasp its meaning for us: the tragic lack of insight, lack of sympathetic understanding; and we have recalled a line from Hannah's song of faith and triumph, "Let not arrogance come out of your mouth." I have tried to point to the desperate need for this lesson in our convulsed social situation.

I regret we can not reflect further this morning on our stampeding sons and daughters in rebellion, mouthing slogans — violent slogans — instigated, in too many instances, by criminal agitators. Time will not permit. It is, further, too large a matter for a preacher to encompass in half an hour. And the pulpit has a basic limitation: it is one-way; it does not give the pew a chance to talk back.

How many broken homes would be saved, how many divorces would be averted, how many bruised friendships would be healed if Eli's obtuseness were recognized and Hannah's sorrows were understood, and her admonition heeded: "Let not arrogance come out of your mouth."

We are now in a election season. Hot tempers and

partisan zeal are rocking our beloved country. Thank God we have the established channels in law to enable every man the right to speak his mind. We shall emerge a stronger, wiser nation, please God, if the citizenry is worthy of the great boon of American democracy and equal to the restraints it imposes. We must not be stampeded; we must not be shouted down. We betray our American heritage, we betray our Jewish heritage, if we mouth the clichés, the slogans of the hour, and do what everybody else is doing because everybody else is saying and doing it. Surely we are old enough to know that because everybody is saying it does not make it good or beneficent. We Jews are a stiff-necked, stubborn people. It is a precious inheritance. It saves us from merciless mediocrity.

I want to close my sermon this morning by citing some wise words spoken by our own good friend, Dr. Abram L. Sachar. Addressing a freshman class at Brandeis University, Dr. Sachar spoke this admonition. If I had the power I would make every young person, every parent, every black man, every white man memorize them as his motto in our day of alarms:

> I would beg of you [students] to look out how you use hard words, proud words. Nailed boots leave scars that never heal, and hard words wear nailed boots. You are going to live among the great issues of your time, perhaps of all time. You will have to fight, in words and actions, for your beliefs. If you brutalize the language of dissent, dissipate the proud words on parochial concerns, what will you have left for the truly great issues? If you cannibalize your adjectives for minor irritations, where will you find a vocabulary for the racists and the demagogues and the termites in the democratic household? [Brandeis University Bulletin, June, 1968, p. 2]

ARROGANCE

In the words of our *haftarah* for this Rosh Hashanah, spoken by a peasant woman several thousand years ago:

> Let not arrogance come out of your mouth.
> For the Lord is a God of knowledge,
> By Him actions are weighed.

7

A Lamp Unto Our Feet (A Memorial Sermon for Yom Kippur)
[5726-1965]

As the years multiply and we move down the corridors of our destinies, gates opening before us and gates closing behind us, the *yahrzeits* in our lives multiply and deepen. No need for little lights when the gates open: births, growth, achievements, love, marriage bring their own cheer. We are on tiptoe; we plunge forward. In the words of the popular song, "O what a beautiful morning; O what a beautiful day! Everything is coming my way!" Thank God for that. Blessed are we who know such stages in our lives. But the corridors wind and turn and inevitably we find ourselves in dark corners. We feel trapped as gates close behind us: advancing years, illness, loss of loved ones, one after the other. Then we need a lamp unto our feet and a light on our way. Blessed are we who do have such a lamp to guide our steps.

That is what the humble yahrzeit candle does for us. It is a light upon our way.

It is sad to note how the tradition of observing yahrzeit has been snuffed out by the violence, the tumult, the raucous vulgarity of our time for many — too many — of our people. We are so busy, so sophisticated, so hard! We pride ourselves on being tough. Who but old fogies kindle little lights in their homes and recite the kaddish in the sanctuary?

The humble little yahrzeit candle has been a beneficent — yes, a redeeming — light in a world choked with smog.

It conserves the memories of our loved ones and illumines our personalities. Observing yahrzeit in our liberal Jewish tradition means recalling our beloved departed and blessing their memories — and being blessed by them.

It does nothing for our departed. It is only superstition to believe that we render our departed some specific benefit. There is nothing we can do for them. They are in a realm beyond our reach. But it does much for the living. I believe it was Maurice Materlink in his little book, "Beyond the Great Silence," who wrote: ". . . we can do nothing for them; it is they who, from the depths in ourselves in which they dwell, can do everything for us."

Yahrzeit observance, the kindling of a light, the recitation of the *kaddish,* are not for the departed; these are for us the living, so that we may hold on to all that was sweet and lovely and good in them, so that we may snatch from oblivion strength and meaning and dignity for our own lives.

You who have laid to rest father or mother, or husband or wife, or child, *and who do observe yahrzeit for them,* know what I mean.

The speeding years rob us of everything — everything we love and cherish. Yahrzeit observance comes from the genius of our people for conserving what we cherish and protecting ourselves from being stripped naked.

Solomon ibn Gabirol was one of our synagogue poets, considered by scholars as the greatest synagogue poet of all time. He belongs in time to the eleventh century, the so-called Golden Age in Spain. Legend has it that he was killed by a jealous Arab poet and was buried beneath a tree. That tree soon began to yield exceptional harvests of luscious fruit.

Our spiritual lives are rooted in the lives of the good and noble loved ones who went before us. Yahrzeit observances — candle, kaddish, yizkor — above all, meditation, reflection, looking within — are our effort to feed the roots of the tree of wisdom and reverence and perspective on our mortality. It is our effort to shield the light in the lamp from being blown out by the coarse winds of vulgarity.

There is the other side to this shield: We not only receive light from those who went before us; we ourselves *are* a light to those who follow us. Our sons and daughters, our grandchildren, husband or wife — when in God's own good time the hour comes to them to kindle a light for us and rise in the sanctuary for the mourner's kaddish — will they find a redeeming light in what we will have transmitted to them?

We cannot buy this light in a supermarket; they will not buy this light. We can only breathe it into them as we live and love and labor with them.

With the Psalmist we affirm:

> Thy word is a lamp unto my feet,
> And a light upon my way.

(Ps. 119.105)

8

The Mistress and the Maid
[5725-1964]

I SHOULD like to lift from the Torah portion for this week one single verse. It carries a tremendous load of explosive freight, like those giant trucks on the highways loaded with gasoline. We pass them with deference, at our own risk. Under certain circumstances, like these trucks, our text can explode and create enormous havoc. It did explode, more than once, and unleashed intellectual-religious-political warfare. It also reveals the depths of human nature and its frustrations. Still more, this deceptive little verse has a double lesson to teach us.

This is the verse, Genesis 16.6. Our Father Abraham is speaking to Sarah, referring to Hagar:

> Your maid is in your hands. Deal with her as you think right. Then Sarai treated her harshly, and she ran away from her.

Notice, first, the depths of human nature revealed here. Recall the Bible story.

Abraham and Sarah were childless, and were advancing in years. There was a haunting void in their lives. Remember the times in which they lived — some four thousand years ago. Historians can only speculate. There were none of the sophisticated compensations we have to still the unsatisfied hungers of life. With childlessness went a feeling of inadequacy and even shame. Women gossiped: Sarah was very beautiful, but she was not all she was supposed to be. God was punishing her.

Abraham and Sarah were frustrated. Sarah was embittered. Naturally enough, like most frustrated women in such circumstances, I suspect, she turned jealous, suspicious, envious, cruel. Abraham was worried. Further, he was a man of substance. Who would inherit his possessions? There was no inkling, as yet, of the beneficent institutions we have evolved for the constructive transmission of our worldly goods in the form of institutions, foundations, endowments, enabling a wise person to perpetuate his name and his influence after death. Only a servant, of an alien people, would inherit his goods; Abraham was dejected. He had left his native land, his home and kindred, to release a new vision in the world. God himself had lured him to do that, and promised to make of him the "father of a multitude of peoples," "like the stars of heaven," like "the sands on the seashore." But he was childless. He brooded over it, and the years were slipping by. He was deeply disturbed.

Sarah had the answer, after a time, in keeping with the standards of the age and the country. If a man's wife was childless, the husband was allowed to take a concubine. We read in Genesis 16: "And Sarah said to Abram, 'See, the Lord has kept me from bearing. Consort with my maid; perhaps I shall have a son [and be built up] through her.'" That was the proper behavior. The child would belong to the first and true wife. The mother of the child, however, was not to be on equal footing with the true wife. She was the "handmaid," or slave girl.

Sarah had an Egyptian servant, Hagar; perhaps we should use the word "slave." Hagar conceived, and then something happened to both Hagar and Sarah. Sarah turned fiercely jealous, and accused Hagar of insolence.

She storms at her husband. (We can make out a plausible case that Father Abraham was a henpecked husband.) Then comes the episode in which we are particularly interested. Abraham turns the pregnant Hagar over to irate Sarah and says: The girl is yours. Deal with her anyway you like. Sarah gives full play to her bitterness and deals harshly with her. Poor Hagar runs away, seeking shelter in the desert. Here we have one of the most heartbreaking, pitiful scenes in the Bible. Wailing by a well in the Negev, she hears a heavenly voice, commanding her to return to her mistress and submit to her authority.

The depths of human nature are plumbed in this story: the frustration of childlessness; the feeling of inadequacy; jealousy and temper on the part of a woman so handicapped; haughtiness on the part of a younger and fruitful woman; dull despair on the part of a good husband caught between too quarreling women; worry weighing down a good man concerned with his worldly belongings after he is called to his eternal rest. It is all so human. That's the stuff of which novels and dramas are made. All reflected in this little, apparently simple, statement on the part of a man to his wife: "The maid is in your hands. Deal with her as you think right."

So much for the humanity of our text. But how is it explosive?

I must take a few minutes to talk on Bible exposition. We cannot read the Bible without a commentary. It is an ancient literature, moving on various levels, reflecting in its language, its metaphors, its idiom, its psychology, in its theology especially, an ancient world, a world far, far behind us. Angels do not walk our earth anymore, unfortunately; they would have a difficult time on our highways. Unlike Father Abraham we can not take a walk with God, nor hold a conversation with Him in the shade of an oak tree. It takes training, imagination, perception in the realms of the divine and the awesome to read the Bible intelligently. Always serious readers of the Bible followed a guide.

Some of these commentators, following the bents of their own minds, sought the simple meaning of the text; or the ethical, moral teaching of the text; or the deep faith embodied in the Scriptures; or the underlying meanings veiled in allegory, in fable, in legend.

A special word about the allegoric method of Bible interpretation: It was developed by the philosopher Philo of Alexandria, first century. He is *the* allegorist in the history of Bible exegesis.

An allegory is a veiled presentation of a truth — an extended metaphor, a figure. The Statue of Liberty is an allegory. Subject the material of which the statue is made to the severest tests and you will not find any liberty or refuge in it. But there she stands, "a mighty woman with a torch," welcoming the wretched masses "yearning to breathe free." It is a powerful allegory.

The story of Jacob and Esau struggling in their mother's womb is an allegory — of two peoples, or nations, predestined to clash for supremacy. The prophet Nathan's little story of the rich man who robbed the poor man of his only little ewe is a powerful condemnation of King David. "Thou art the man!" The allegoric method is a valid method of interpreting Bible text — when applied accurately, where it belongs, not used promiscuously.

Philo has had an enormous influence on the Church and the Mosque, more than on the Synagogue. The rabbinic masters were careful never to apply the allegoric method to law. Let your accountant, or lawyer, apply the allegoric method to your contracts, or income tax returns, and you see at a glance how dangerous a method it is when misapplied.

We return to our text: "The maid is in your hands. Deal with her as you think right."

Following the allegoric interpretation, Sarah is no longer a woman of flesh and blood, the wife of a man named Abraham; Sarah is now the true faith, God's own revealed truth, and she is mistress. Hagar is no longer an Egyptian wench; Hagar is now the servant of the true, the only legitimate mistress. Hagar is what we today call the sciences, the humanities — secular learning in all its branches.

Professor Harry A. Wolfsohn, in his masterly work on Philo, quotes one of the Church fathers (Clement of Alexandria) expounding our text as follows: "I embrace secular culture as youthful, and a handmaid, but thy (that is, the Bible's) knowledge I honor and revere as the true wife."

Sarah is the mistress; Hagar is only an alluring wench, who must be subordinated to and disciplined by the mistress.

This is highly explosive. We recall one major explosion that took place in the sixteenth century. The echoes are still reverberating.

Galileo is recognized as the father of experimental science. He argued, you remember from your school days, that the earth revolved around the sun, that the earth was not the center of the universe as affirmed in the Bible. The Inquisition cracked down on him. He was contradicting the Bible. He was tried and found guilty.

That is, Galileo was Hagar, insolent to the mistress. The Church, Sarah, demanded conformity and submission. Has not God Himself commanded Hagar: "Go back to your mistress and submit. . . ."?

A parallel case in Jewish history is the excommunication

of Spinoza. Spinoza contradicted the revealed teachings of the Torah.

Our text exploded in another area — in the area of Church-State relations and human rights.

As the mistress, the Church is the custodian of God's revealed truth and His eternal will. The State is Hagar; Hagar must submit to the mistress. The State is here to serve the Church and follow its will. Pope Innocent III (12th–13th century) put it in another metaphor, another allegory: The Church is the sun; the State is the moon. The moon shines by the reflected light of the sun. Bible proof? The story of Sarah and Hagar, allegorically interpreted.

The battle is on today, and will continue as long as men differ in their thinking and in their beliefs. Thank God for the wall of separation between Church and State in our American democracy; thank God for the First Amendment to the Constitution of the United States. Our Israeli brethren have no such protection against religious tyranny; they are under constant strain.

From Jerusalem come persistent reports of conflict between Synagogue and State. Matters of education, marriage, divorce, abortion, autopsy, public transportation on the Sabbath, are in the news daily. The Minister of Social Welfare — a member of the Israel Cabinet — is summoned by a rabbinic court to justify his role in advocating military service for women from religious families. Think of a member of our American Cabinet being summoned to justify his policies before Catholic or Protestant or Jewish ecclesiastics! A member of the Israel Supreme Court must travel to New York to be married to his fiancée by an American Rabbi because she is a divorcée and he is a *Cohen*; primitive rabbinic law prohibits such marriages.

I received a call from a man at whose wedding I officiated thirty some odd years ago. Could I help him?

His son lives in Israel, and must produce a certificate testifying that he is Jewish and born of parents who were properly married, according to strict rabbinic law. I had to explain to my friend that my certification would only damn him; I am only a Reform Rabbi, which is anathema to the Israel rabbinate. I suggested that he advise his son to take his bride to Rome, Athens, anywhere, and be married by the local Rabbi.

Synagogue and State are feuding. Involved are the rights and liberties of millions of people, and probably most of these do not believe in the major doctrines and practices of the rabbinic hierarchy. Israel will never achieve a free democracy until it has learned from us the American principle of complete separation of Synagogue and State.

We have noted the deep humanity reflected in our little text, and recalled its explosive nature, allegorically interpreted, as seen in the conflict between revealed religion and reason, and Church-State relationships. What shall we learn from this?

We have a double lesson before us.

First, we must be on guard against spurious interpretations of the Bible. "Bible Exegesis" sounds bookish and far away. There is religious-cultural-social explosive power in Bible exegesis. We Jews have been branded as the Cain of mankind, the curse of God resting upon us and our children forever, on the basis of an allegoric interpretation of the Cain and Abel story. Spurious Bible interpretations sanctioned the burning of witches, condoned slavery, justified race segregation. The Mormon Church, basing itself on a Bible passage, has it as a religious dogma that the

Negro is an inferior race, so decreed by God. Beware of fanciful Bible interpretation.

Second, we need both Sarah and Hagar. "Then Sarah treated her harshly, and Hagar ran away," reads the Bible text.

Sarah — organized religion — can be, often is, frustrated, embittered, vicious in her intolerance. That only leads the Hagar of science and secular learning to run away. And Hagar can be an irresponsible wench, ill-tempered and intolerant. We need both the insights and disciplines and sanctities of religion, and the insights, the skills, the visions of the sciences and the secular humanities. It is too late in history to belabor this point. Science is not all-knowing, does not have the final answers: too often it is only skill and technology, making and dropping atomic bombs without conscience. We need both: the wisdom of the ages and the vision of the Kingdom of God on earth, and the liberating insights, the skills, the daring of the sciences and the secular humanities. Neither Sarah alone nor Hagar alone; we must have both, but each in her own domain, with a decent respect for the other.

And both must heed the prophet and his admonition: to do justly, love mercy, and walk humbly with God.

9

A Prayer for Our Country
[5728-1967]

I INVITE you this morning, gathered as we are in prayer on Rosh Hashanah, to reflect with me, and to think with me, in terms of our relationship to our country and our nation. We are gathered as religious Jews, as individual men and women, as a historic Jewish people, and as American nationals, in response to the ancient summons to remember, and make firm resolves, as our fathers did before us across the centuries and across the countries. We are part of an ancient people, witnesses to an ancient faith; and we are, also, part of a mighty nation "conceived in liberty and dedicated to the proposition that all men are created equal." We are Jews, religious Jews; we are also Americans, loyal Americans. We would be responsible Jews, and responsible Americans. We are the heirs to Moses and the Prophets and Psalmists and the martyrs; we are the heirs also to Washington, Jefferson, Lincoln. We cherish the Ten Commandments, and we cherish the Constitution of the United States and its Bill of Rights. Ours is a double heritage, one fortifying and giving meaning to the other: Hebraic faith and American democracy.

Our country is in acute travail today. Our cities are battlefields. More than fifty of our heavily populated cities were rocked by racial violence this past summer. We are caught in the crossfire of racial warfare. The warning of our rabbinic masters has come true once again: warfare, they said some two thousand years ago, comes upon the world because justice is delayed, and "because of them that make wrong decisions."

Our country is also deeply mired in faraway jungles. We are pouring fantastic treasures and much — the God of mercy help us, too much — blood into the endless swamps and jungles of Asia. We are deep in the valley of decision — desperate decision.

Angry voices — voices of hate, many of them, and voices of treason, too many of them, and voices of earnest sincere and intelligent men — have created spiritual tumult. The choices before us are horribly confused. Reason is muffled and the lights are flickering.

Our country is in a desperate hour. We American Jews are searching our hearts along with all thoughtful Americans. We search our hearts this morning as a Jewish congregation, as an *American* Jewish congregation, as sons and daughters who love our country, and we pray for the America we love. A prayer of penitence and a prayer for wisdom and integrity rests on my heart this morning. I want to share it with you.

Every Sabbath and every holiday morning a prayer for our country is spoken in our synagogues. This is an ancient ritual, in obedience to the teaching of our talmudic masters, formulated some eighteen–nineteen hundred years ago. Our version of this prayer begins, you recall: "Fervently we invoke Thy blessing upon our country and our nation." Tremendous drama is packed into the little word "our" for those of us who are familiar with our history and with our liturgy. "*Our* country and *our* nation."

Compare this prayer with the prayer for the governments our fathers and grandfathers and all the generations behind us spoke for *their* governments. I give you a literal transla-

PRAYER FOR OUR COUNTRY

tion of the prayer for the government spoken by the grandparents of some of you within the hearing of my voice. In fact, this pocket-size *siddur* I have in my hands belonged to the grandfather or great-grandfather of one of you. One of our congregants gave it to me some years ago. (Grandchildren do not treasure their grandfathers' prayerbooks; they give them to the temple as rummage):

> May He who grants salvation to kings and power and dominion to princes . . . May He exalt and crush their enemies under their feet, and *May He implant rahamonus [pity, mercy]* in their hearts so that they may have pity upon us and all Israel [Jewry] . . . [Then follows a petition for the salvation of Zion, our true home.]

Notice:

First, Our fathers' prayer is for *rahamonus* — mercy, pity, that God place pity in the heart of the Czar, or Kaiser, or Prince, so that he may deal mercifully with his Jewish subjects. They were at the absolute caprice of their rulers. *Second,* they prayed as aliens, as subjects. They had no rights, no liberties within the law excepting as their rulers saw fit to grant them any rights. They were vassals, literally the property of their rulers, for them to exploit any way they saw fit.

When the Jews of the Rome ghetto, for example, petitioned the Roman Senate for the privilege of remaining in their rat-infested, plague-ridden alleys along the Tiber River, the Jewish representative would literally place his head at the feet of the Senator, who would literally place his foot on the head of the Jew, and grant the petition or not, depending upon the fee the Jewish community would pay. It took centuries of blood and tears and frightful indignities to give us equal rights, or rights within the law.

The United States of America is the first country in

history to give us equality of rights and liberties guaranteed by the basic law of the land. The United States of America was the first country in the world to convert us Jews from the "Wandering Jew," the accursed of God, branded as the "Christ killer," doomed, like Cain, to wander the face of the earth as a fugitive, into a free citizen, with all the rights and liberties and dignities of a free citizen.

No country in history has given us the opportunities America has showered upon us. Our sons and daughters are in every college and university of the land, on the faculties as in the student bodies; they are in every industry, in every legislature and court of the land, from the humble municipal courthouse to the Supreme Court of the United States. We are bringing our talents, our brains, our industry, our visions into every laboratory, every institution, including the United Nations, where the son of a humble Russian Jewish peddler represents our country in dignity and in honor.

Do we pray for *rahamonus* as the grandfather who owned this prayer book did? Are we scraping and crawling on our bellies before the entrenched in power?

When I hear youngsters in our own congregation sneering at the prayer for our country, I feel sick at the pit of my stomach.

Permit me to rehearse a personal story.

A dim vision of my early childhood comes to me when I reflect upon the tirades against our country mouthed by our so-called Jewish intellectuals, a generation that knows not and remembers not Kaiser nor Czar nor Inquisitor. I see my father, deep in the shadows of childhood memories, holding in his limp hand a white sheet of paper and weeping. It was a letter from someone informing him that his daughter, her husband and two small children had been murdered in a pogrom somewhere in Russia, on Easter

Sunday, in celebration of the risen Christ, Prince of Peace! The next Sabbath, I am sure, my father went to synagogue and there he recited *Kaddish* for his slain and heard the prayer entoned asking God's favor upon the Czar and for *rahamonus*.

How can we transmit to our super-intellectual sons and daughters, raised in an opulent, permissive society, the enormous reality in the simple words, *"Our* country and *our* nation?" The Bible speaks a powerful warning to us American Jews: "When Jeshurun grew fat he grew thick and forgot . . ."

I was deeply disturbed last winter when I worshipped in a number of temples on successive Sabbath mornings. The prayer for our country was invariably dropped. We must abbreviate and save time, and so the Rabbi omits what he considers least meaningful. (*mini* services; *mini* sermons!) In one temple I found this prayer — page 148 in our prayerbook — entirely pasted over with some mimeographed material.

It pains me to criticize colleagues. I do respect their intentions and their courage. They would be unworthy of their rabbinical robes if they did not speak their minds fearlessly. But the steady drumfire of criticism of our President, of our highest authorities, creates the impression that it is hostile talk by hostile, not adequately informed, critics. Sincerity and good intentions are not enough. The issues that beset our country are too complicated — issues in foreign affairs, in military strategy, in economic matters. They require expert understanding, and our experts are by no means agreed. Too many of them are as befuddled as you and I are. Even young men in pulpits do not know all the answers to all the problems all the time!

More, there is altogether too much invective, too many

personal attacks, too much blind dogmatism in the name of liberalism. A Negro Civil Rights leader, so called, has recently denounced our President at a political rally as being another George Lincoln Rockwell. That is the voice of the lunatic fringe in the Negro community at the moment. But a rabbi is not far behind this lunatic fringe when he called our President another Antiochus. Our Sunday school children know that Antiochus of the Hanukkah story is in the category with Haman and Hitler.

Is that "liberalism"? Is it "prophetic Judaism"? And he spoke in the name of all of us in the seven hundred or so Reform congregations of the land and abroad. Sheer, unbridled, brash irresponsibility! Yes, "when Jeshurun grows fat he grows thick..."

A free pulpit — and thank God we do have free pulpits in most of our Reform temples — makes at least two demands: *first,* adequate information, adequate knowledge; *second,* a sense of responsibility. "Ye wise men," the talmudic masters teach us, "be heedful of your words."

Last July 27 the President of the United States called for a day of national prayer. Civil war was raging in two major cities of the land at the time. The following Sunday was set aside as a day of prayer for the nation. Where were we Rabbis? On vacation! Our synagogues? Closed. Vacation. That obtained everywhere in our city and throughout the land, with some solitary exceptions. A *minyon* here and there for the few mourners who observe *Kaddish.* I went to Sabbath service that weekend in a neighboring community. The Rabbi had not one word of reference to the national crisis and the President's proclamation. He is a child of our time who has not known Czar or Kaiser.

I watched the newspapers, our local newspapers and the New York *Times.* The *Times* reported one Rabbi in all of New York as having conducted a special service. There may have been more — I profoundly hope so; but only one was reported. Protestant ministers and Catholic priests were reported. Locally, only one Rabbi — heading an association of Orthodox Rabbis — was quoted. And all he said was, "It is incumbent for every Jew to pray for the peace of the land in which he dwells." This dictum goes back to early Talmudic times when Jews by the thousands were literally crucified by their Roman overlords.

The land in which he dwells! Is the United States of America only a land in which we happen to dwell? Or, is it *"Our* country and *our* nation?"

There is a prayer in my heart this Rosh Hashanah morning on behalf of our country. I am sure it expresses your feelings as it does mine. As it forms itself in my mind it is a two-fold prayer: a prayer of atonement, *al chet,* for the sins we have sinned in our relationship to our country; and a prayer of rededication and renewal of devotion, a profession of faith in our country.

A prayer of national contrition for our national sins we as an American nation must speak, for — in the words of our prayer book — "Yea, we have sinned, we have transgressed, we have done perversely."

We as an American nation have not done justly, have not loved mercy, have not walked humbly with our God. We have exploited and dealt treacherously. Our involvement in Vietnam is a bitter, a colossal tragedy. We have been dragged into the jungles of Asia by world forces, by international politics, not because our President, nor our Secretaries of State and Defense, are evil men. We may be sure there is not a soul in Washington that is not sincerely, ardently, trying to find a way of disengaging ourselves. I am one of those who believe that we should disengage ourselves completely, as speedily as possible. The question is, How?

But talking pacifism will not help us. We must never forget that unilateral pacifism is national suicide. More, unilateral pacifism will bring on war.

Incidentally, what shall I say to your son or grandson who comes to me with a paper in his hands asking me to attest to his pacifism? He is a conscientious objector, he tells me, and expects me as a Rabbi to attest to it. With a heart full of compassion for him I must speak the stern truth: Judaism is not a pacifistic religion. Think of the State of Israel last June 5, and how tremendously relieved all of us were when Israel vanquished its enemies. Remember the Maccabees.

There is a second part to our prayer for our country, and that is reaffirmation of faith in our country, faith in its genius for self-government, in its dedication to justice and to freedom, faith in its President, its Legislatures, faith in its courts, faith in its police — yes, faith in the police, despite the local miscarriages of justice in times of crisis. We deplore "police brutality" and police corruption wherever it may manifest itself; but a time when firemen are risking their lives putting out fires set by insane men and are shot at by snipers, is no time to undermine respect for police authority.

We speak a prayer of confession and contrition. Our civil war, our race insanity, is not due to willful evil on the part of our leaders. Again, "warfare comes upon the land when justice is denied and because of them that make wrong decisions." We are in the throes of the same Civil War that scorched our country in the days of Abraham Lincoln. For a hundred years and more since Lincoln signed the Declaration of Emancipation have we been stoking the furnaces of race injustice. We are reaping the whirlwind. We imported human beings, enslaved them, and bred them as animals are domesticated and bred. Mothers, unknown fathers, children sold and scattered across the land. Now we complain that their offspring have no family feelings and no sense of responsibility to their own. For a hundred years and more, and for some two hundred years before then, we kept them out of our neighborhoods; now we complain that they make bad neighbors. We have denied them decent schools in their rat-infested tenements and ghettos and complain that they are ignorant, shiftless, criminals.

All these crises require historic perspective. They are terribly complicated. There are no simple answers. It is inevitable that we differ. We have every right to differ, and every right to speak our minds in and out of our pulpits, in and out of our pews. But let us remember Jefferson. Paraphrasing him: on the burning issues of the day — Vietnam, race warfare, civil rights, poverty, open housing — we may differ; but we differ rationally, as loyal Americans who love our country and respect our duly constituted authorities. And if we are mature men and women we will realize that none of us has the final answers, and therefore we must indulge our mutual inadequacies.

We have loudly proclaimed our ideal of equality, but, as someone expressed it last summer, what does equality mean if all of us are equally rotten? The "fast buck," self-indulgence in the name of self-fulfillment, pleasure at all and any cost, at any and all times, canine morality — we are in a moral morass. "Yea, we have sinned, we have transgressed, we have done perversely."

Ours is the same America that has gathered the oppressed, "the wretched refuse," the homeless, and given them the opportunities to make of themselves free and proud citizens, in peace and in honor and in loyalty. Is there a better hope in all the world than our Constitution and our Bill of Rights? Is there any other country in which we would rather live and raise our families?

This is a time to reread Lincoln: "The dogmas of the quiet past are inadequate to the stormy present. The occasion is piled high with difficulty, and we must rise with the occasion. As our case is new, so we must think anew. We must disenthrall ourselves and then we shall save our country."

A Russian Jew — perhaps a blood relation of some of us here this morning — Elias Lieberman — wrote his profession of faith in America a generation or so ago. I believe it is our profession of faith in *"our* country and *our* nation":

> I am an American.
> My father was an atom of dust,
> My mother, a straw in the wind,
> To His Serene Majesty.
> One of my ancestors died in the mines of Siberia;
> Another was crippled for life by twenty blows of
>   the knout;
> Another was killed defending his home during the
>   massacres.
> The history of my ancestors is a trail of blood,
> To the palace gate of the Great White Czar.
>   [Were he writing today he would recall the Nazis
>   and Auschwitz, of course]
> But then the dream came —
> The dream of America.
> In the light of the Liberty torch,
> The atom of dust became a man,
> And the straw in the wind became a woman,
> For the first time.
> "See," said my father, pointing to the flag that
>   fluttered near,
> "That flag of stars and stripes is yours;

PRAYER FOR OUR COUNTRY

It is the emblem of the promised land.
It means, my son, the hope of humanity.
Live for it — die for it!"
Under the open sky of my new country I swore to do so;
And every drop of blood in me will keep that vow.
I am proud of my future.
I am an American.

10

Pollution — of Heart and Mind
[5732-1971]

"POLLUTION" is the master word of our time — perhaps the crucial word of our generation. God's good earth — of which the Creator said, according to Scripture, "Behold, it is very good!" — is ravaged. Our fields and our forests are plundered; our lakes, our rivers are open sewers. Daily we read in the newspapers of fish washed up on the shores, choked by the refuse of man's doings. On the Pacific coast last winter we watched men desperately trying to rescue sea birds trapped in oil spills. The poor creatures could not move their wings nor their legs, their feathers pasted into casts, crushing them. Man, "the crown of Creation," as we are conceited enough to believe, with his guns and his poison sprays, belching chimneys, racing motors — on land and sea and in the skies — fills the atmosphere with soot. Glorying in our murderous skills, we are exterminating the birds of heaven and the animals of field and forest. We are spending vast sums — and that is only the beginning — in attempts to save ourselves from the relentless pile-up of garbage and poison, searching for clues to our redemption from man-made filth.

Why speak of such an unpleasant subject on Rosh Hashanah? We are gathered for prayer, for meditation, for the solemn music of our faith, for the comforting words of our tradition, for a bit of reassurance of a merciful

Presence presiding over our destinies. Why speak of pollution? garbage? refuse?

Because, my friends, it is not only our earth and air, rivers and seas, not only our streets and parks and cities that are polluted; our hearts and our minds are polluted. The hearts and minds of our children and of the generations still in the womb are contaminated. Recently I read a study warning us that infants may come into the world addicted to drugs, to alcohol.

Our Hebraic heritage affirms — *has* affirmed for centuries through prophet and sage — that God made man of the earth and endowed him with a vision of and capacity for the eternal, and commanded him to be God's co-worker on earth in fashioning a world fit for human beings to dwell in. Our masters have proudly taught this to the generations, with the admonition to "choose life and live, you and your offspring." We rehearse this in the Torah portions for the Days of Awe. The meaning of the shofar sounding is peculiarly real in our day: "Awake, you sleepers, and ponder your deeds."

I watch the youngest member of my family — a two and a half year old grandnephew — play with a noisy contraption his doting grandfather gave him. It is supposed to be a helicopter, makes a racket — wheels revolving, lights flashing, crashing against chair and table legs. The child babbles (only his mother understands him). He imagines his arm broken, his chest crushed, his head smashed — a two and a half year old playing in his innocence. We condition our children to violence early. I read a report recently of toys built in the forms of guillotines, time bombs, hypodermic needles!

Our streets, our highways, our parks are crowded with roaming bewildered youngsters — *our* children, *our* grandchildren — unwashed, unkempt many of them, no joy in their faces, no sense of direction in their roaming. They do have homes; they do have families; loved ones waiting for them, brokenhearted. They are on the road. On the road! What is driving them? Some are "finding themselves," we say by way of trying to comfort each other. Looking for what? They know not; we know not; no one knows. Black cats looking for other black cats in dark alleys.

Some are bleary-eyed. The Lord of mercy help us. Drug addiction is the Black Plague of our generation. All the while we send men to the moon, lavishing astronomic sums, and claim we have no adequate resources to maintain clinics for our sick children.

Our campuses are battlefields. Thank God things seem to be quieting down just now. Is it the calm before another storm? Who knows!

The pollution of heart and mind is ominous. Coarseness, boorishness all around us; the tides of vulgarity are inundating us. I watched a young man the other day sprawled out in his streetcar seat. Standing before him, literally hanging over him, were two aged women with bundles in their arms. It never dawned on this unkempt young man to offer one of them his seat. Such barbarism is symptomatic of degeneration in our life as a society.

We entered on our worship for the Days of Awe last night with the haunting words of the Psalmist:

> I lift mine eyes unto the mountains.
> Whence shall my help come?

My help, *my* — first person, singular.

> (Permit a digression. I was enormously impressed, as most of you must have been, when I heard on the radio one of the Apollo 15 astronauts report his sensation as he stood on the moon — *on* the moon, mind you — and facing the

mountainous formations heard in the eternal silence the voice of the psalmist: "I lift mine eyes unto the mountains.")

"Whence shall *my* help come?" If we are at all religious, if we are responsible men and women — as husbands, as wives, as parents, as Jews — Jews, heirs to Moses and the prophets — as American citizens, heirs to Jefferson, Lincoln, where shall we find relief from the tides of vulgarity that are inundating us, our homes, our schools, our synagogues, our country? All of us are contaminated; all of us need redemption. Rosh Hashanah is the time to think responsibly in terms of *heshban hanefesh* — taking inventory of ourselves, of what we have been doing with our lives, and what we have been doing to the lives of those entrusted to us.

Certain infections come into our personalities naturally, inevitably. They are peculiar to human nature.

Say our Rabbinic masters: hatred of fellow humans, anger, envy ("blowing your top," as we say), a grudging disposition, nursing grudges, hunger for revenge, never forgetting hurts, real or imaginary, "take a man out of the world." That is the rabbinic idiom for shortening life.

I recall a man saying to me some years ago, "If I as much as suspect someone of offending me, I never forgive him." Think of living with a man like that, or doing business with him, or associating with him socially or in communal endeavor. Think of all the poison that builds up in his personality and what it does to him.

But on this Rosh Hashanah morning I am inviting you to think with me of the special sources of infection that are corrupting our generation. In view of the clock on the wall, I must limit myself to three major sources of pollution.

First, Vietnam.

We must lift ourselves above political partisanship in appraising the calamitous effects of the Vietnam war on our young, on our nation morally.

Some fifty thousand young men slain; thousands upon thousand crippled, blinded; thousands returning home with venereal diseases, thousands drug addicted — an appalling legacy of evil to bring to their young wives, their children, and to children yet unborn. The sins of the fathers do afflict their children unto the second and third generation, as Scripture warns us. Think of the thousands and thousands of youngsters brutalized, embittered, cynical, aimless, frightened lest they be drafted. An awful legacy of obscenity.

We pray for the mercies of God to rest upon our nation and help us achieve a measure of redemption. We cannot pull out of Vietnam too soon.

The *second* major source of pollution I wish to consider with you this morning is the temper expressed in the *now generation — now,* immediate gratification, no thought of tomorrow, no yesterdays and no tomorrows in our thinking, in our planning, in our living. Basically, it means life without perspective and without a sense of responsibility to anyone, not even one's self, not even one's loved ones.

Instant familiarity, instant love, instant sex — and instant divorce, if there is a marriage to begin with. Instant success — no patient, honest work, no serious planning, no "long dreams of youth," no earning, no achieving. That takes time. By the time many of our sons and daughters leave high school they must have all the experiences of life.

Has anything fine, anything beautiful, anything beneficent ever been achieved in one fell swoop? How may we transmit to our restless sons and daughters the truth that work, perseverance, infinite patience, often tears in the night, are the price of success in any worthy endeavor? And

POLLUTION — OF HEART AND MIND

how may we transmit to them the meaning and the reality of the word "worthy"?

How many tries did the Curies make before they found their radium formula? How many tries did Dr. Jonas Salk make before he found the formula that wiped out poliomyelitis? We marvel at the fantastic achievement in landing men and equipment on the moon and bringing them back safely. Why do not our newscasters stress the months and years of research and efforts of thousands of patient, dedicated scientists in achieving this?

Not only instant success, instant gratification, but instant wisdom as well. Listen to some of our smart, glib young people proclaim in boundless omniscience final judgments on which the keenest minds in history pondered for years and reserved judgment! Instant solutions to vastly complicated problems centuries in the making!

And instant success in marriage. The permissive psychiatrist and smart lawyer are ready with their skills to effect a divorce.

One of the lovely practices we have at Temple Sinai Sabbath worship is inviting members of the congregation to come before the open ark and speak a word of thanksgiving for all God's mercies to them in the course of their years together as husband and wife. I am always deeply moved when I see a couple deep in years come up to the *bimah*. Sometimes my impulse is to take them by the arm and help them up the several steps. And I always regret that there are not more young people in the pews to watch them. Is there any better way of meeting the sunset of our lives than together as husband and wife? I am sure there is not a couple that has not known trials and tribulations of all sorts, and even shed tears in the night. Instant success in marriage? Lord of mercy, forgive our moral, our spiritual myopia.

Of course, we can, and many do, go to the other extreme — postpone living, tomorrow and tomorrow and tomorrow! So pass the years away!

A dear friend, who has since gone to his eternal rest, told me a story of a colleague of his. This man would not take the days off allowed him; he saved them and saved them; he would retire a year earlier. The poor man never lived to enjoy the year.

Of course we can, and many do, go to the other extreme. We save and save for the rainy day; we save for our children and grandchildren, as if they needed it. Some of you will recall the oft-quoted words of Hillel, "If not now, when?" But to the impatient pagan who would be taught all of the Torah while he wobbled on one foot, Hillel, wise teacher that he was, did give the quick answer, but promptly added: Go home and study. One must reflect, absorb, assimilate, achieve perspective if he is to gain a measure of wisdom. That takes time, and more time.

Basic in Jewish moral thinking is the Golden Mean — not one extreme and not the other, but somewhere in-between. Maimonides urged it in his time, back in the twelfth century. And that is characteristic of the good common sense in Jewish thinking. "Good deeds as such are equi-balanced, maintaining the Mean between two equally bad extremes, the too much and the too little." The good life is balanced between extremes.

Just where is the line between the *too much* and the *too little*? That is the secret we must learn for ourselves. Nobody can dictate it to us. Wise teachers, wise religion, will help us find it.

The *third* major source of pollution corrupting our generation that I would discuss with you this morning is permissiveness — permissiveness, anything goes, in the home, in the school, in our social life, in our business life, even in our religious life. No standards. Standards restrict; the idea of standards is old-fashioned. Are we not liberals?

Liberalism is a precious concept; liberalism has freed us from tyranny in government, in religion, in the intellectual life.

Basically, liberalism means an open mind versus the cramped, cruel, everlasting "No!" In government it has given us democracy; in the intellectual life it has given us science; in religion it has given us the right to follow the good and the true as God gives us the power to see the good and the true. It has liberated us from primitive superstition of all sorts and set us free to follow the finest visions of prophets and sages of all peoples of all times.

To turn liberalism into vulgarity and promiscuity is tragic. The fact is that not everyone has the mental capacity nor the character to be a true liberal. Liberalism assumes men and women of principle and refinement. Liberalism is not for slobs.

I hear people say, condoning every foolishness, even sheer stupidity, of their young, "as long as they are happy!" My friends, we are not living in Shangri-la; Adam and Eve were expelled from the Garden of Eden a long time ago. We are not placed on earth to enjoy! enjoy! We have work to do, loads to lift, pain to assuage, evils to banish, duties to discharge — as sons and daughters, as husbands and wives, as parents, as citizens. *Enjoy! enjoy!* as the main dynamic in life is not for decent human beings.

My friends, when venereal diseases and hard drugs are corrupting our children of high school — even junior high school — age, it is no time to practice promiscuous permissiveness in the name of liberalism.

We used to talk of conscience, of character, of "character education." Have you heard the term "character education" at your parent-teachers meetings recently? at your school committee meetings recently? The major emphasis seems to be "Keep the kids happy!" And they are so sated with happiness that they are bored to extinction and cop out!

I have spoken of three major sources of pollution corrupting our generation: Vietnam, the *now* temper, unbridled permissiveness. There are many further sources of contamination that must be considered most seriously: the fast buck; immoral advertising and huckstering rousing greed; irresponsible news media exploiting every form of sensationalism; garbage literature and theatre exploiting psychotic sex. We have not the time this morning to consider these as we should.

Where shall we look for relief from these evils? "Whence shall my help come?"

There are no absolute answers. No man has the final answers to our moral problems. Beware of the man who urges final solutions in familiar slogans. But I am convinced of the directions we must take to find the answers.

We must bear in mind where the answers are not.

The answers are not in "the good old days." We need not devote any time to this point. Long, long ago a Bible sage affirmed: "Say not: 'How was it that the former days were better than these?' It is not out of wisdom that you inquire concerning this."

The answers are not to be found in clichés, catchwords, shibboleths. Beware of simple answers glibly spoken.

The answers are not in harsh discipline of the past. External discipline will not win for us the confidence of our young.

I would emphasize two points in choosing our direction where we may hope to find answers to help us in our need.

First, we must take a long, critical look at our educational theories and practices. We are worshipping blindly too many sacred cows.

At a dinner party recently a friend, who teaches history in high school, proclaimed proudly that he tears things apart in his classes; he rips off the legends, the myths, the popular notions. George Washington, by the time he is through with him, emerges a first-class bounder. All this nonsense about his sterling character, his integrity, his dependability is legend appealing to simple minds. I asked him, as quietly as I could, "After you have debunked, and pulled apart, and analyzed, and exposed every bit of pretense and sham, what do you put together? What do you give your children that they may respect, and by which they may be guided decently?" I don't think he heard me.

We teach our children to pull things apart, to expose, to analyze. Good. Granted. Of course. But when do we teach our young to put things together into some coherent bit of wisdom by which they may live honorably?

And why are we confusing technical knowledge and verbal fluency with an appreciation of goodness, loveliness, reverence — yes, reverence? We teach our junior high children how babies come into the world. Good. We should. But are we giving them a sense of morals in the matter?

A second sacred cow: We must realize that moral, spiritual salvation can not be achieved by intellect alone, by technologic education alone.

James A. Michener expresses it fairly in his book, "The Quality of Life." He writes: "We need neither Catholic answers nor Quaker, neither Moslem nor Buddhist. We do not need answers dictated by ritualistic preference of one religion as opposed to another, but we do want answers derived from the inherited experience of mankind, and these are most often found in religious teachings."

For us Jews the answers are found in Judaism as a religious discipline, with its vision of the eternal and the enormous emphasis on personal and family integrity.

I pray that we Jews be discerning enough, that our synagogues and our schools and our homes be intelligent enough, to recapture the moral strength that has distinguished us as a God-fearing people.

Say our masters: of all the animals man alone is created with a straight backbone so that he alone in the animal kingdom may walk erect, his head high, his eyes raised to the mountains, whence comes our help.

May the blessings of God rest upon all of you — your children, your homes, your synagogues, your country — and may He grant all of us the strength and the skill to achieve a good year.

INSTITUTIONAL

11

Dedicating a Synagogue

The Congregation of Temple Sinai was dedicated on September 10, 1939, housed in temporary quarters on Sidlaw Road and Commonwealth Avenue, Brighton, Massachusetts. Five years later, its present sanctuary and school house were dedicated on Sewall Avenue and Charles Street, Brookline. The following excerpts are from the address of dedication on September 8, 1944.

YOU and I, my friends, have reared a new synagogue, at a time when synagogues without number have been pulverized in the historic centers of Jewry. And we have reared this synagogue on America's generous earth, under America's peaceful skies, part of the very landscape of America. Praised be His Holy Name. That is the way the synagogue has risen from its ashes, like the phoenix, age after age, and achieved immortality.

This is the hour of our success. The word I would speak, first, is a prayer for deliverance from the perils of success.

Success is strong wine. It turns many a head and perverts many an institution. Success may blunt conscience.

A wise Christian teacher is quoted as saying that when a new cathedral is dedicated with pomp and glory and self-righteousness, the devil moves in and opens his own private chapel. Success has profaned many a shrine, in Jewry and

Christendom alike. When Jeshurun grows fat he grows thick and scorns God who made him.

It takes character and practical idealism to carry success gracefully. Institutions, like certain men, grow hard, arrogant, scornful of others. And so, tonight, as we are dedicating our new synagogue, we pray that He grant us the vision and the intelligence to keep alive the flames of the sacred even in this brutal age. God grant us the courage and the wisdom to look to our success not in numbers, not in buildings, but in our integrity as a congregation dedicated to the Holy One of Israel.

Second, I repeat tonight what I have been saying repeatedly these past years: Temple Sinai is a Jewish religious congregation, dedicated to the progressive interpretation of our ancient faith. We have taken the name "Sinai" because Sinai symbolizes the Moral Law. To the Moral Law, as understood in our Jewish tradition — particularly in our prophetic tradition — are we dedicated. We shall have no other gods.

We are a body of Jews who are devoted to Judaism as a religion — an ethical, moral discipline of life in terms of God, Torah, Israel, in the deepest and broadest interpretations of these areas of Judaism. And this Judaism is not frozen, not congealed, not corked up in ancient bottles. Ancient our Judaism is; nevertheless, vigorous, young, forward looking; respectful of historic forms and traditional sanctions, we nevertheless refuse to be hypnotized by the past.

And we do not consider ourselves in exile. We are a living organic part of the American nation. We are at home — completely at home — on America's rich earth, under America's spacious skies, and thank God for our double heritage of faith and freedom. Today we are shedding our blood and tears — along with all other Americans — in the effort to defend and preserve our "last best hope of earth," even as we did at Gettysburg, even as we did at Valley Forge.

Nothing in Judaism and nothing in Jewry is alien to us. Every movement and every institution honorably championed by honest men shall have our sympathetic but critical appraisal. We reserve for ourselves the right to think through every issue and to follow the right as God gives us to see the right.

I have been saying repeatedly, and I repeat tonight: Temple Sinai is above party. We steadfastly refuse to become a tail to anybody's kite. We refuse to become a tail to the Zionist kite. We refuse to become a tail to the anti-Zionist kite. We refuse to be stampeded by the hysteria of the hour. We refuse to become a sounding board for anyone. We shall continue as a congregation, please God. Our pulpit shall remain a religious pulpit, not a soap box. Our school shall be a nursery of religious idealism, not a propaganda center.

This emphasis was made constantly from the Temple Sinai pulpit, as, for instance, on Yom Kippur in 1958:

> Let us buy Israel bonds, let us invest in Israel; but Judaism is more than Israelism. Let us travel to Israel and let us send our sons and daughters there for study and for enlargement of their Jewish horizons and the deepening of their Jewish loyalties. But Judaism is more than that — much more, and without this *more* we perish as a people. Remember that eighty-six percent of us are outside Israel, and will continue to be citizens of our various countries wherever we are — please God!
>
> Our life and the length of our days is where it has always been: in *Torah*; more specifically, in the Synagogue as the heart of Jewry; more specifically still: in our Jewish learning, our Jewish observance, our Jewish duties — keeping the

Sabbath as best we can, observing the Holy Days and Holidays, saying our prayers, blessing our children at Bar Mitzvah, at Confirmation; marrying them in their faith, enriching our homes with our Jewish books and symbols and prayers, saying Kaddish for our dead, and Yizkor for our loved ones and martyrs, rejoicing in our freedom, uniting with all good men of whatever faith, or of no faith, in insuring the rights and liberties of all men, striving for the Kingdom of God on earth where and when none shall hurt nor destroy, and where all men shall live in peace and honor and there be none to make them afraid. All this spells our Judaism.

Jewry, today, is badly divided. For the most part all our arguments and all our mimeographed resolutions — the latest plague afflicting us — are ancient. We debated these ideologies in one form or another in ages past.

An old *midrash* reports that one day the prophet Elijah was walking down the street of a certain town when a highly-agitated scholar of the Law approached him and said, Master, I am greatly worried. Some of my colleagues say that what is most important in Israel is Israel (or, as we would say, the nation), while others argue that the most important matter in Israel is Torah (or, in the language of our day, religion). I am greatly perplexed. I am devoted to both and know not which to choose. Elijah replied, the all-important matter is not Israel as such, and not Torah in itself. The all-important matter is a consecrated Israel. That is, in our vocabulary, not Israel the race is what matters, and not religion in the abstract, disembodied of the living, suffering, striving community; the all-important matter is Israel as a God-fearing community.

A consecrated Jewry, a God-fearing, morally-responsible Jewry — that is primary, that is the all-important matter. Everything else is secondary, which we should pick and choose in keeping with the dictates of our free and honest minds. Upon this solid rock we stand.

Temple Sinai is a free and liberal Jewish congregation. Ours is a free pulpit and a free pew. No one dictates. No one dominates. No one dictates the teaching nor the preaching.

The synagogue, throughout its long career of more than twenty-five hundred years, remained dedicated to Torah rather than to the shibboleths of the hour; to the Lord of all rather than to the idolatries of race, or blood, or nation. In the hour of crisis it had to draw on its moral reserves and decide: "In the strife of Truth with Falsehood for the good or evil side."

> Thus saith the Lord:
> Let not the wise man glory in his wisdom,
> Neither let the mighty man glory in his might,
> Let not the rich man glory in his riches;
> But let him that glorieth glory in this:
> That he understandeth and knoweth Me,
> That I am the Lord who exercise mercy,
> Justice and righteousness in the earth;
> For in these things I delight,
> Saith the Lord.
>
> (Jeremiah 9.23)

12

A Heap of Witness
[5705-1944]

"Come now, let us make a covenant, you and I; and let it be a witness between you and me." So Jacob took a stone, and set it up as a pillar. And Jacob said to his kinsmen, "Gather stones," and they took stones, and made a heap; and they ate there by the heap. Laban called it *Jegar-sahadultha* [Aramaic, a heap of witness], but Jacob called it *Galeed* [Hebrew, heap of witness]. Laban said, "This heap is a witness between you and me, when we are absent one from the other . . ."

(Genesis 31.44–49)

THESE words were spoken between Jacob and Laban. There was bad blood between the two men. Both had engaged in sharp practice; both regretted it. Now they were taking leave from each other. They sought to seal a compact of good faith. In keeping with the practice of the time, they erected a monument in the form of a heap of stones. Laban, though a cousin of Jacob's, was a Syrian. He therefore called the heap *Jegar-shahadutha*, which is the Aramaic for "a heap of witness." Jacob called it *Galeed*, the Hebrew for "a heap of witness."

It was good practice among Bible folk to attest a covenant of good faith, or to mark a victory, or to express gratitude, by erecting a monument. Many such monuments have survived to our time. The practice is still universal.

A HEAP OF WITNESS

Tonight is Rosh Hashanah. We are assembled in prayer, as a congregation in Jewry, in the house of God, along with the millions of our people the world over. We are renewing our covenant with our God and our covenant with our people. Long ago have we sealed this covenant. In every age, year after year, have we renewed it. Of course, this year our sons and daughters are scattered over a flaming globe. But, be they in the jungles of Asia or in the ruined cities of Europe, in submarines at the bottom of the seas or in bombers above the clouds, few of them will not give some thought to the fact that tonight is a sacred night in Jewry; few will not feel deep longing to be with their own in the house of the Lord. And, of course, a deep loneliness is in the hearts of most of us here tonight, as in the hearts of those in every synagogue on the face of the earth. We need not arouse feelings that most of us have struggled very hard to master. These feelings are sacred. Let that rest between every lonely heart and the Father of Mercies.

Tonight we of Temple Sinai are witnessing anew the ties that bind us to our people and our God in a special sense. We are greeting the new year in our new house of prayer. Temple Sinai stands dedicated in our community as a new heap of witness. You and I — all of us here tonight — have called this new synagogue into being. It is infinitely more than a heap of stones, lovely as it is. A synagogue is "a heap of witness." A synagogue is a symbol — symbol of something tremendously precious in our life as a Jewish people. "Come now, let us make a covenant you and I, that there may be a witness between you and me."

Temple Sinai stands as "a heap of witness." A witness to what? I devote the sermon of the evening to a statement of the vision that guides us as a congregation in Israel.

First, Temple Sinai stands as a witness to the fact that

we are Jews, God-fearing, morally-responsible, reverent Jews, as does every synagogue in the world.

We are Jews. We are one living community held together by sacred ties. We have a long past, which we would not escape even if we could; we have a common and painful present, which we dare not avoid; before us is one unfolding future, which we face together with courage and high hope.

We are an ancient people with long memories. We are not sprung from the head of any Zeus. We are not like Jonah's gourd, sprung up in an instant, and therefore likely to perish in an instant. We are not self-made. Behind us are many generations; above us is the God of our fathers, He who called the ages into being. We are the children of countless yesterdays. That gives us perspective, meaning, dignity. That gives us, too, moral dynamics for today and tomorrow.

To forget our yesterdays is to live, work, and think in a vacuum. Basic knowledge, sound logic, valid values cannot be sucked out of our own thumbs. We must be in communication with the long experiences of our people — with the prayers of the psalmists, with the visions of the prophets, with the teachings of the rabbis, with the moral power of our law givers and our martyrs. The tricky double-talk of our propagandists, the high-pressure salesmanship of our professional saviors may be spicy food for our people addicted to sensationalism; but that is not the stuff to sustain us in health in difficult times. Certainly it is not the stuff to sustain Judaism as a moral power in the world.

Too many of our spokesmen and our leaders have just discovered the fact of Judaism. They are impassioned zealots of one or another tangent of a majestic system of thought and idealism. Like the blind men and the elephant, they are groping in the dark, mistaking one or another detail for the whole. Some decent appreciation of the treasures of our people and our faith would restore balance.

We are in a common present, whether we like it or not. The truth spoken by our ancient masters stands: *yisroel arevin ze boze* — Israelites are responsible one for the other. All Israelites know one fate. The world about us with its sledgehammer blows fuses us into one, even if we would sever ourselves from our brethren. In the slaughterhouses of the Nazis, in the sealed cattle-cars of Germany, before the firing squads in Hungary, Jews were not asked whether they were Orthodox or Reform, whether they were Zionist or anti-Zionists, whether they were rich or poor. They were Jews, and they shared the same fate.

I am not belittling the differences among us. Some of these differences are basic and tremendously important. They are championed by honorable men, who differ honestly and frankly. We have nothing to fear from honest differences held by intelligent and good people. Out of the clash of opinions, truth comes into the world. The unfortunate fact is that there are narrow bigots in every camp, opportunists who would build careers for themselves on the miseries of Jewry. There is a lunatic fringe around every movement. They are the ones whom we should fear.

But beyond all our differences is one solid reality which we ignore at our peril, and that is that we are one people, one historic community, however we define it. We have been one people for a great many centuries; we are one today; we are facing the future as one.

And we do have a future — a bright future, a future with healing on its wings. Israel has often been compared to the phoenix — that sacred bird in Egyptian lore that crumbles into ashes on the altar, only to rise reborn from its own dust, to live for a long stretch of time, to be consumed again and to rise reborn once more, on and on, all through the centuries, forever. That is an apt description of Jewry's experience in history.

We are links in a mighty chain. We of this generation are not the last link. If we are in the depths of a dark night, we must brace ourselves with the conviction that every night gives way to a new morning. "I shall not die but live and declare the glory of the Lord." As long as we say that in sincerity, we are invincible and immortal.

Past, present and the dawn of tomorrow merge into one reality — a reality that absorbs all our arguments and all our divisions and makes us one. We are Jews. From Ankara, several weeks ago, came a newspaper report which illustrates this truth:

> ANKARA (JPS) — Many thousands of Hungarian Jews who in recent months were baptized to avoid the Aryan laws, which at first seemed to be aimed only at those professing the Jewish faith, are now relinquishing Christianity and returning to the faith of their fathers, according to the official organ of Hungarian Jewry, Magyar Szideklatia.
>
> Within the past two months, 9,745 Jews returned to their ancestral religion, the newspaper states.
>
> Partners to mixed marriages, children of mixed marriages and others, entitled to privileged treatment and even exemption from ghetto internment, have refused to avail themselves of these opportunities and declared themselves willing to share the common fate of all Jews in Hungary.
>
> (July, 1944
> *Jewish Advocate*)

Thus Temple Sinai stands, I pray to God, as a heap of witness testifying to the fact that we are Jews. In the *second* place, Temple Sinai testifies to our unswerving determination to think and act above party.

"Parties," said Dr. Solomon Schechter, "come and go,

but the word of our God shall stand forever." We are a congregation. Ours is a synagogue, and the synagogue is the heart of Jewry. Nothing that is real in Jewry is alien to us. We are not only free but are duty-bound to think and speak on any issue that may confront us. I stressed this point in my sermon of dedication two weeks ago. We need not enlarge upon it now.

Temple Sinai stands as a witness to a *third* ideal in our life: it testifies to the sacred in human life.

We are in the vise of a secular, noisy, and brutal age. We are in an age of robot planes. Beastiality such as only diseased minds ever imagined has become the daily experience of countless thousands of human beings. The conscience flickers faintly; it has gone out altogether in vast areas of the world.

The primary contribution that Judaism has made in history and which it must repeat with new power in our time is the integrity of the sacred in human life — the integrity of the sacred in the life of the individual, in the life of Jewry, in the life of the larger humanity. Our fathers called it "the fear of the Lord." That is the beginning of wisdom and recently we were reminded that we have too much cleverness and too little wisdom. The synagogue stands dedicated to the life of conscience.

From its earliest days at Mount Sinai, Judaism has championed the sovereignty of the Moral Law. Not race, not tribe, not brute might, not the Moloch of the Sovereign State, not blood and not soil, but the Moral Law is the foundation of the world. *Olam chesed yeboneh* — the world is planted in loving kindness, avers the Psalmist. Upon three principles does the world rest, say our Talmudic sages: Upon justice, upon truth, and upon peace. That is, the Moral Law is sovereign. All else is idolatry.

Man holds something of the divine in him. Even the

brutalities of war and race exterminations can not eradicate it. Beyond and above us is the Holy One, blessed be He. Our fathers spoke of *kiddush hashem* and *kiddush hachayim* as the primary business of religion — the sanctification of life and God. "Whoever takes one life," say our rabbinic masters, "is as one who crushes a whole world." In an age of exterminations, lying and killing beyond the grasp of the normal imagination, it sounds naive. Naive or not, it is the hope of the world. It rests on the conviction that there is a God, that there is something sacred in human life. The synagogue — I pray that our synagogue no less — testifies to the integrity of the sacred in human life and in human affairs.

We Jews have the proud privilege of championing the sacred in a prostituted humanity.

Temple Sinai testifies to a *fourth* conviction. We American Jews are an organic part of the American nation. We are not an alien block in the stream of American democracy. We are not here temporarily. We are not here with any mental reservations. We are not in exile. We are Americans. We treasure our American heritage fully as much as does any other strand of the American nation. We came here with Columbus, we bled with Washington at Valley Forge, we wept with Lincoln at Gettysburg. We shall remain here as long as the sun shines on America.

Our Temple building is in Colonial tradition. That is fortunate. I know that you are as happy about it as I am. It is symbolic of the fact that we Jews, with our Synagogue as the basis of our separatism, are native to the American landscape.

We are told that hard times are ahead and that prudence dictates that we prepare another home for ourselves. Let's not pack our bags yet; let's not think in such panicky terms. We proceed on the conviction that we are here forever.

I know — and you know — that many centers of Jewry that have felt themselves rooted and secure were uprooted and banished, or destroyed. Some there are among us who are constantly pointing to German Jewry as a horrible example. We can not tonight enter into an analysis of the validity of the thesis. But there are at least two considerations that I should like to point out, however briefly.

One is that it is a surrender to fatalism and despair to say that because it happened before it must of necessity happen again, that because it happened in Spain or in Poland or in Germany, it must happen in the United States. We Jews are not fatalists. That is why we have survived. We are basically optimistic and forward looking. Our Golden Age is ahead of us, not behind us. The sociological, political, economic, ethnic facts that made for the misfortunes of Jewries at various times in different lands do not obtain in the United States. And there are new developments in history, and mankind does grow, and civilization does progress, despite the horrible collapse of civilization in our time. Just because it happened before does not mean that it must happen again.

The other consideration against the argument that we Jews live with our bags packed is that, granted that we American Jews are in danger, granted that what has happened to German Jewry is likely to overtake us, our acceptance of this tragic possibility does not mean that we are to build bridges for our retreat. What it should mean is that when that evil hour comes we shall be strong and determined and organized to fight for our heritage as Americans — fight with all we have and are, with no thought of retreat, fight like brave soldiers, and if we go down in defeat, we go down with the conviction that from our blood and our tears America will arise reborn as the land of the free and the home of the brave, and in that reborn America our children's children will find peace and security, even as our fathers found under the stars and stripes.

"This country belongs to the people who inhabit it," Lincoln averred. We Jews are among those who inhabit it. We shall not compromise; we shall not retreat; we shall not cower. We shall claim our heritage as valiant soldiers, worthy of Valley Forge and Gettysburg. We have shed our blood and the blood of our children so that America may continue as "the last best hope of earth." We are not planning to surrender in advance of the fight. Any other adjustment on the part of the American Jew towards the evil day that is prophesied for us is defeatism, and treason to America herself.

Our sons have not shed their blood in the deserts of Africa or the jungles of Asia or on the beaches of Salerno or Normandy so that we may live in America temporarily, nor that we may live here as an alien element. We are here; we have earned the right to be here for our children and our children's children, forever.

Temple Sinai, with its traditional American architectural form, blending into the New England landscape, stands as a witness that we Jews are Americans, at one with and inseparable from the American nation.

"Come now, let us make a covenant, you and I, that there may be a witness between you and me."

A witness to what? A witness to the eternal fact that we are Jews, loyal, God-fearing Jews; a witness to the fact that we are above party; a witness to the sacred in the life of man and mankind; a witness to the eternal covenant that we have sealed with the American nation — one and indivisible!

God grant us the calm courage, the detached wisdom, and at the same time, the militant strength to stand unrushed, refusing to be stampeded. And God grant that this synagogue that we have reared shall be a true *Galeed*, a heap of witness to all that is sacred, so that through us something of the prophet's vision may be glimpsed:

> So thou, son of man, I have set you a watchman unto the house of Israel; therefore, when you shall hear the word at my mouth, warn them from me.

13

*Thy Vows Are Upon Me, O God**

MINE is the duty of the heart, at this sacred hour, of speaking a prayer and repeating my vows — a prayer of thanksgiving, and vows of rededication.

The values and the ideals basic to the covenant into which you and I have entered have been stated — stated reverently, thoughtfully — by my brother and teacher, Professor Samuel S. Cohon. Once again I am deeply indebted to him. That he feels generously rewarded for his trouble in coming to us tonight I am certain. For him, as for me and mine, and as for all of you, I believe, tonight is a Sabbath of the soul.

It is gracious and kind of our new friend, Dr. John M. Ratcliff, to come to us to share in the program of the evening. I anticipate with much delight cooperating with him and his faculty in bringing to the students of Tufts University something of the sacred wisdom and prophetic vision of our heritage, so desperately needed in our time, particularly by young, groping minds.

What I must say to you tonight — *must* because of an inner compulsion — despite the lateness of the hour, has been said by two ancient poets, whose words are preserved

---

* March 29, 1946, at special Sabbath eve services, installation to life tenure as Rabbi of Temple Sinai.

in the Psalter. I place these two verses before you with the briefest possible commentary. They convey the sacred burden of sentiment far better than any words of mine possibly can.

Chants the Psalmist:

> *Thy vows are upon me, O God;*
> *I will render thank-offerings unto Thee.* (56.13)

"Thy vows are upon me, O God." That is the real meaning of the rabbinate. That is the primary impulse in the life and labor of the Rabbi — if he is worthy of his high calling. You have been encouraging me in every way to be true to my vows. The covenant we are sealing tonight is the climax of a great many deeds of loving-kindness you have shown me. What you are saying to me is, "Be a Rabbi; be true to your vows as God gives you to understand your vows. We don't expect you to be a successful promoter in ecclesiastic big business; we don't expect you to be a propagandist of vested partisanship; we expect you to keep off the bandwagons. We expect you to be a Rabbi; we expect you to be true to your vows." For me to do less would be to commit a grave sin.

When I was ordained Rabbi the words of the prophet Malachi were spoken by the head of the Hebrew Union College, Dr. Julian Morgenstern:

> The law of truth is in his mouth,
> And unrighteousness is not found on his lips;
> He walks with me in peace and uprightness,
> And turns many away from iniquity.
> For the priest's lips should keep knowledge,
> And they should seek the law at his mouth:
> For he is the messenger of the Lord of hosts.

I am not presumptuous enough to say that I have fully lived up to this exalted conception of the true religious teacher. I can say that within my limited capacities I have tried to keep the ideal before me. You have helped me keep the vision. You are enabling me to repeat my vows.

I repeat my vows, again in the words of a Psalmist:

> I will walk within my house in the integrity of my heart;
> I will set no base thing before mine eyes. (101.2)

Many are the base things that are afflicting our household of faith; careerism, worldly success, popularity, raucous secularism, omniscient pontificating, blind partisanship, half truths, clichés, clichés, and more clichés. We need not enlarge on these tonight. I ask you to join me in prayer to the Holy One of Israel that *our* synagogue be spared these base things. I ask you to unite your hearts with mine in prayer.

> I will walk within my house in the integrity of my heart;
> I will set no base thing before mine eyes.

14

Dedicating a Schoolhouse: Plant Your Sapling

On November 1, 1968, the congregation of Temple Sinai dedicated its schoolhouse to Rabbi Beryl D. Cohon. The following paragraphs are excerpts from Rabbi Cohon's response to the main address of the occasion delivered by Dr. Abram L. Sachar, Chancellor of Brandeis University. Omitted are the purely personal matters.

NOW, what is all the excitement about this evening?

A name is affixed to a schoolhouse of a modest synagogue. The name of the schoolhouse is not particularly important; the name after the title *Rabbi* is not important at all. What *is* important — supremely important — is that it is a schoolhouse, a Jewish religious schoolhouse, the right arm of a Jewish congregation, and a Rabbi: that is, school, synagogue, Rabbi. This is of supreme significance in our life as a covenanted Jewish community. Here is the formula of "the eternal life He hath planted within us."

Doctor Sachar, distinguished historian that he is, will bear me out, and I have affirmed this conviction over and over again from this pulpit. Except for the Jewish communities that have been annihilated by fire and sword, any Jewish community, anywhere on earth, any time in history, that has dissociated itself from the synagogue perished and has been forever erased from the book of Jewish life; any community, anywhere on earth, any time in history, that has stood true to the synagogue has survived the ravages of the ages, and is alive, flourishing intellectually and spiritually, this day — after centuries of Crusaders, Inquisitors, pogrom gangsters, Nazis, Communists. I affirm this as an unshakable truth of Jewish history. The words Moses spoke many, many centuries ago, and which we rehearse in our synagogue worship, are literally true: *v'atem hadveykin b'adonoy eloheychem chyim kulhem hayom:* "All you who have been steadfast in the faith are alive, each one of you this day."

This conviction as the formula for our immortality as a Jewish people has stood the test of the centuries; I urge that ultimately it is the only formula for our survival as a worthy, meaningful Jewry anywhere in the world. I am not negating anything else. I am for every Jewish organization, every Jewish institution that is maintained by honest Jews honorably: social, philanthropic, educational, cultural, in any language, on any ideological base. Israel reborn is, of course, of supreme importance. Of course! But with Yehuda Halevi I affirm, "The synagogue is the heart of Jewry."

That is what we are affirming this evening with the dedication of a schoolhouse to the honor of a Rabbi. If it helps mobilize and energize a congregation, it is good.

We are living at a time when the life and work of Yohanan ben Zakkai acquires enormous significance. Son of the first century, he lived through the destruction of the state and the national shrine. All had gone up in flames to the torch flung by the Roman general. Jerusalem was choked with the rotting bodies of Jewry. Insane zealotry annihilated what had escaped the Roman Legions. Disease, starvation, insanity were sweeping the Holy Land; countless thousands were carried off to the slave markets of the

DEDICATING A SCHOOLHOUSE

Mediterranean. Sixty thousand Jewish slaves perished in the building of the Roman Colosseum. (We pull up in our tourist buses, look around, click our cameras and dash off to the next sight.) Jewry, knee-deep in its own blood and tears, was on tiptoe, watching for the coming of a heavenly messiah to redeem them. And messiahs came, only to plunge their people into more tragedy.

Yohanan ben Zakkai, meantime, had lifted himself out of the ruins, retired to a village on the Mediterranean, gathered around himself a number — a very small number — of scholars. From this obscure group came a new application of the Torah to the new circumstances, a new meeting of the new challenges, a new authority. You and I today as Jews, as Jewish congregations, owe our life to Yohanan ben Zakkai.

Time will not permit me this evening to draw a parallel between the destruction and the messianism of the first century and that of our own time. It is obvious, if you reflect on it for a little while, and equip yourselves with the basic facts. The millions slain by the Nazis, the millions crushed as Jews by the Communists, our centers of learning, our academies, our synagogues annihilated, we — we in this blessed land — are the *she-erit yisroel,* the saving remnant, in the Diaspora. The most poignant recollection I have of the first years of Temple Sinai is listening to the horrifying reports of Hitler's hoards annihilating city after city, synagogue after synagogue across Europe. We — in an old house on an obscure street in Brighton — were building a new synagogue. The phoenix was coming to life under our own hands. Will you permit me to dream, in all our sophistication, that in God's own good time I may bring this recollection to the Academy-on-High and report it to Yohanan ben Zakkai!

Yohanan ben Zakkai turned a deaf ear to the messianic

frenzies of his day. He toiled over the Law and taught, and taught, and taught, and raised disciples, patiently, lovingly, prayerfully. It is written in the Talmud in his name to this effect: If you have a sapling in your hands and someone announces, "Look! The Messiah is approaching!" go on with your planting. Only after you have planted it go out to receive the Messiah.

All our brilliant slogans, all our technologic devices, all our isms — all our clichés — well, only after we have taught the students we do have, made the best use of the time we do have, faithfully, lovingly, prayerfully, may we abandon ourselves to the excitements of the messianists in our midst, hailing from Madison or Park Avenues.

Plant your sapling. Build your school. Teach. Teach your teachers. Teach your parents. Cultivate your synagogue life. Here is our life and the length of our days as Jews, and "may He establish the work of our hands; yea, the work of our hands, O Father, establish Thou it."

Epilogue: "I Am the Synagogue"*

I AM the Synagogue.

I am the heart of Jewry. I have shielded you for more than two thousand five hundred years. Through all these cruel ages, swept by wrath of fire and sword, I nursed you with the word of God, healed your wounds with the balm of faith, steadied your minds and fortified your hearts with the vision of the Eternal.

When your fathers wept by the waters of Babylon, I came into the world, summoned by their need; whenever they were in the valleys of many shadows, under the heels of the pirates of all ages and all lands, I gave them loving asylum. In Babylon and in Persia, in Greece and in Rome, in the face of the howling crusaders and in the clutches of the black Inquisition, in the pogroms of Poland and in the concentration camps of the Nazis, I have been, and by my presence brought the living waters of the Eternal to the parched lips of your fathers. When the world derided them, I restored them: When men cursed them, I blessed them.

---

* With reference to the Synagogue attention is called to the present author's *From Generation to Generation,* Introduction, "The Two-Cent Candle and the Pearl," p. 11 ff. (Boston, 1951), *My King and My God,* Supplement: The Rabbinate, p. 217 ff. (N.Y., 1963).

I am old and I am young. I am older than the memories of the historians; and as young as the youngest child.

I bring you peace by teaching you duty. I sanctify your lives with holy seasons. I preserve your heritage. I make the faith of the fathers the faith of the children. Behold, a good doctrine do I give unto you; forsake it not.

> — From pageant
> FEASTS OF THE LORD (1944)